Forward

A true story of fast cars, fast girls, gang fights, drugs and God.

I am a guy who likes action and adventure movies like the Bourne series or "The Fast and the Furious." Sometimes when watching these flicks I would reflect, "my teen life was like this only true, I should write the story." So I set out to put to print the many high speed car races and car wrecks and fights and times with hot girls into a fun read that would also include how I met God at the wrong end of a 357 Magnum pistol and how that event impacted my life. I am the storyteller son of a great storyteller so I really just wanted to tell the story. I couldn't really tell this crazy story without telling the story so I decided the book would be the uncut version which is rated R for drugs, sex, and violence.

I have told this story to thousands of people in 36 countries and I can provide a PG version that is more appropriate for certain audiences. I am not trying to glorify my poor decisions but it is my sincere hope that this uncut version will relate to someone living in the fast lane on the ragged edge like I was. To someone who can't find the brakes or the off ramp. I am hoping this will direct you to the off ramp.

A wise man learns from his/her mistakes but an even wiser man learns from the mistakes of others. While bad decisions can make good stories it is also my hope that some may learn from my abundance of bad decisions! And also from the very good decision that became my off ramp into a much more sane healthy life.Your life will be a collection of your good or bad choices. *While the stories are true some names have been modified to protect the identity of the individuals involved.*

TABLE OF CONTENTS;

I dedicate this book to my amazing wife Mary Jane Torion Willows and my kids Josiah - check out his music on YouTube under Jasia, Esther , Abe & Lester our pooch !

Opening Scene

1981 Whitefish, Montana; On a cold January night past midnight in the middle of main street.

A glossy black Chevy step-side pickup with monster tires pulled up and the driver demanded that I and my five mates tell him where Todd was. Todd was my friend that dealt Coke and these crazed dudes were obviously out to revenge a deal gone bad. They had blood in their eye so neither Scott nor I told them of Todd's whereabouts. (Even though we had just left his house.) They seethed when I evaded their question and the driver got out aggressively and yelled "you punks better get the Hell out of here and quick!" Danny Seliger reflects that one of them got out and started waving a large pistol around at this point. I was pretty tough and didn't run from hardly anybody, especially when Scott was at my side, so I strode calmly out into the middle of Main Street and squared my shoulders like Wyatt Earp to meet them. Their leader had white skin and long black hair. An athletic build and the look of a guy who liked to fight and usually won. As he walked up to meet me our eyes locked in combative disdain. I noticed he was older and bigger than I but that had never stopped me before. He grabbed me by the collar and pulled back his fist to nail me. I glanced behind him to see his massive hulking side-kicks waiting to assist him; one of them had a big bore pistol aimed at my head...... (should I stop there....)

When I turned to face him I imagined that Scott would be on my right and my other 4 friends would be behind me ready to rumble. To my alarm I glanced around and my friends were no-where to be seen! .....the gun must have scared them off.   I quickly decided, "this is no time to fight, this is a time to talk...and fast." I said, "Why don't you just let me go, I'm not the one you are looking for." He let me go and being a little too drunk and stoned I stupidly leaned over to pick up my fallen Stetson party hat. As I was coming up with it I saw his fist flying toward my face......

Chapter 1   A Son to be Named

My father James Lake Willows came to Montana in 1934 to Homestead 644 acres near Fairfield Montana. Dad was a cheerful, courageous, hard working man. My mother's real name was Olga because she immigrated from Latvia before Hitler's invasion. I remember Mom trying to hide the fact she was at least 20% Jewish. Their first child was a brown haired beauty named Sharlon Linda Willows. Next came a winsome cheerleader named Bonni who married an equally winsome stage personality named Rob Quist. To compliment the good looking Willows girls a beautiful strawberry blonde came later in Dad's life. By then he wanted a son to name James so badly that he named the girl Jamey.... almost a James! Then on March 9, 1963 Jim and Laverne Willows finally got their beloved son James. I was the beloved spoiled only son! The only drawback was having 3 laser tongued older sisters tease me re-
lentlessly. Once Jamey teased me so badly that I picked up a 7' by 7' pine board and threw it at her in the back yard. It caught some air and boomeranged left going through our dining room window! We love each other though and **worked hard at our Dad's Huckle-berry Restaurant since we could walk !** :) But we were happy and always had money !

I have very sweet memories of being 3 and 4 years old when I would get up and find my beloved plastic hammer then spend time riding my bucking horse on springs. It was hard to pinpoint when my peaceful play days turned into a nightmare of my Mother and Father fighting but by age 5 my parents dinner time civility was replaced by high volume hostility. My favorite escape was the forest and river.

3

pics from left to right, top to bottom;
Mom & Dad
Uncle Rob & I

Jamey, sister Sharlon, and I

Bonni

Sharlon, my niece Willow, Jamey, I, and Bonni

Chapter 2 Mountain Boys

Growing up in Hungry Horse Montana before the dawn of video games was a great adventure. There was an area about a mile walk from home called "The Monagan Holes." It is located at the confluence of the South Fork of the Flathead and the Flathead river.   Huge "Monagan" crane/diggers were used to scoop out tons and tons of sandy gravel to build the Hungry Horse Dam with. Since there were no environmentalists in those days after the cranes were done there were two huge vacant holes. Water from nearby rivers filtered through the gravel and filled the holes making two sizable ponds that were full of snakes, tadpoles, beavers, Loch Ness Monster suckers, and everything a 7 year old boy loves!

I was an ace fisherman by age 4. I practiced casting in my back yard till I could place my lure within a few feet of where I wanted it. At age 5 someone took me down there and I cast my 3 inch long shiny spoon into the green water. To my delight a gutsy 5 inch long shiner chased my 3 inch long spoon down and I caught him! I don't know whether the fish was trying to feed or trying to mate but it was sure fun to catch! From that day on I pestered my Mom daily to let me go fishing down there. Dad knew I had a calculating confident head on my shoulders so he let me do things early in life. He had me cultivating land on our Ford tractor at age 5 and he would let me go fishing alone at the same age. Probably because he grew up like Tom Sawyer fishing Sturgeon on the Snake River from a young age and wanted me to enjoy the same life of adventure. But Mom always said, "not by yourself Buddy." So I lured the kid who lived in the next block to go with me. His name was Jimmy Grant and by age 5 1/2 Jimmy and I were down there almost every day. The real thrill was that we discovered suckers up to 2 feet long in the pond.   5

Me on horse in Lincoln, MT.   Blood Brother Jimmy Grant

When all we ever caught were 4 to 10 inch perch and some shiners these behemoth suckers were royal trophy's to us. We spent days watching them suck along the steep rocky bank then we would carefully position our worm in front of the slow vacuum cleaners. Once every day or two their rubbery lips happened to go over our worm and bingo! They were not too bright but if they saw your worm they might go a foot or so out of their way to suck it up. When they did the fight was ON!!! Bob Lietz and I boiled one up after catching it while we were camping. Boiled sucker with no spice was about the grossest thing I ever ate! We almost gagged and never tried that again! Jimmy and I loved to chew tobacco, He liked Skoal before I converted him to Copenhagen. One evening we decided to see if the Perch would like it. After we caught them we would give them a huge chew then take a small stick and ram it down their throat then release them. 30 seconds after release they would go crazy and come jumping out of the lake swimming all over like a motorcycle that had

6

unseated it's rider. It wasn't very nice but we weren't very nice either. We shot anything that moved and many things that didn't.

 But there were wholesome memorable times too; Like the day Jimmy and I spent all day building the greatest fort that ever existed. We chose a remote Aspen on a secluded hill then meticulously framed a web of Aspen branches 7 inches apart. We then cut wads of grass for the next 4 hours which we meticulously thatched into a roof. When we were done it started to rain real hard and to our satisfaction we stayed inside it without it leaking for an hour or two. We kept talking about what we should name our extraordinary creation. We decided it had to be champion something because it was a fort without equal. Then we recalled how we found a small owl skeleton near the main structural tree. So we christened our fort "Champion Owl." Jimmy and I became blood brothers one day by slicing our palm and mixing the blood to-gether.   Champion Owl was just one of our many little secrets.

The craziest thing that we ever did at the Monagan hole is when streaking was big in the early seventies. We boys all camped under the big birches and after we split about 3 beers somebody decided we should all go streaking. We stripped and all ran along Hwy. 2 for a few blocks in the warm summer night. We thought we were pretty radical and the occasional passing tourists proba-bly wondered what form of strange animal they were be-holding that night!

Dad was a friend of many a Native American person and one came by with a little red fox he wanted to trade for some Jam and gas money. Dad thought it was cool so he made the trade and I became the proud new owner of a 3 month old red fox. I called him foxy! The coolest pet ever. But some real bad dogs came by where we had foxy tied up and chased him under the Volkswagen pickup. At first we thought foxy would be ok under there but one sly hound weaseled its way under the truck and clamped its strong jaws around foxy. Dad was a trained fur farmer and did his best to save the animal to no avail. I was inconsolable! But by and by I began dreaming of my own dog. And began saving every penny I made working as a dishwasher. So when I was that perfect age for a boy to have his own dog, 7 or 8 I think, I got the pick of the litter from my friends Chesapeake Bay Retriever

pups. I felt so elated as I observed the amazing pups. I didn't really make the pick but one of them decided to pick me. The biggest funny looking but handsome chocolate colored pup came running up to me and started biting my shoe laces! I guess it was love at first bite because from then on Grizz my dog and I became inseparable friends! Grizzley turned into 100 pounds of muscle and adventure and could not wait till I got off school everyday. He would come charging out and jump up on me putting his paws on my shoulders with the biggest smile on his face! He was well known in town as a lover, fighter, and personable pain in the butt but people loved him all the same! And so did I.

In those days no-one kept dogs on a leash in Hungry Horse and when people he didn't care for came walking or riding a bike past the Willows place Grizz would come charging out full bore and full bark. I am sure it scared the daylights out of people so I chained him up but he broke every chain I could find. So Dad and I build an 8 foot high solid plywood enclosure for him. He howled non stop till one day he burrowed out to his role as free king of Hungry Horse. He would fight any comer then one day a dinosaur proportioned Great Dane came to town. I knew Grizz would get killed so I ran with desperation to intercept him as he charged at the Dane looking like a poodle next to the monster. Sometimes I would have to hit him with the spare cleat of my snowcat to get him off a dog!

The most dangerous thing that happened to me there was when a friend and I put the snowmobiles away for the season and grabbed our fishing poles then went down to see if the ice was off yet. It was late March or early April. The ice had melted off the end of the second pond so I got in my birthday suit and jumped in! The spring sun consoled my shocked body! We fished for but never caught a sucker, then my mate and I and my sturdy 100 pound Chesapeake named Griz started ambling along the shore in the direction of home. Griz loved to fetch anything so I kept side-arming rocks out onto the shiny ice. Griz roared after them and came back proudly with the rock in his mouth. After he fetched a few I winged a rock out far and Griz dashed after it only to plunge into the water where the ice had rotted. At first it was no big deal as we just called him to come to us. But after 20 minutes Griz was moaning plaintive desperate howls. After 25 to 30 minutes he started to totally lose energy and looked like he would soon drown. I could not sit idly by and watch my best buddy die. I was bundled up in my winter coat because after swimming I was cold. I figured the coat might keep me warm in the frigid water so without taking off my coat or boots I ventured out onto the ice to save him. When I got to where Griz was I fell in too. The coat and boots became like a lead wrapper drawing me to the bottom ! I strug-gled with all my sinewy toughness but the slippery wet ice pro-vided no handhold and though I treaded water desperately I felt myself fighting a losing battle against the frigid watery grave. My friend was an excellent swimmer and he stripped down and came out with the branch of a sapling extended toward me.

9

It was enough for me to grab in order to hoist myself up onto the smooth clear ice. As I did I pulled him in! But he used his great swimming abilities and lack of weighty clothing to get himself out. I think he saved my life and will always be thankful to him for that! By then the will to live was subsiding as Griz barely kept his head above water. I cussed profusely one moment but called out to a God I didn't believe in the next minute! God was probably confused; shall I damn it? Or save the dog? Together my buddy and I desperately heaved boulders and logs out onto the ice till we gradually broke a channel to shore by which my frozen dog could finally struggle to shore. Although it was warm out for so early in the year we both felt hypothermic as we stumbled up the long hilly trail to my house. A hot bath and a warm blanket never felt so good!

My Dad was a fearless man but even he always said I could have easily died that day.

A millionaire from California bought the large acreage called "The Monagan Holes" and made it only theirs with high fencing and "No Trespassing" signs. They bulldozed all the little hills where "Champion Owl" sat till the whole rugged playground looked like a California golf course. They poisoned our beloved perch and suckers and planted trout which they dutifully forbade us from fishing. Even my dog Griz was buried in the sand 'neath a dominant Fir tree where we liked to camp but they told us we couldn't go there anymore. They turned it into a campground, naming it "Flathead River Ranch." They put up about 8 signs to lead tourists to their lair. I'd be damned if I was gonna let these Californicators take away my turf. (I don't feel that way now but as a Montana native some of us carried a grudge toward outsiders.) Clarence Purdy made great spare tire holders for pick ups that he welded in front of the grill and front bumper. Not only was it a great place to store the spare but it was a good deer and brush guard too!

(Also handy for pushing your buddy's truck out of a mud hole.) By now Jimmy and I were driving and every Friday night after a twelve pack of Oly we discovered that the spare tire holders on our trucks also worked great for plowing down the hated signs! (We also found our shotguns worked good for their street lights.) Finally we had pushed every sign down several times except for the huge sign out by the Hwy. 2. After plenty of beer we got my dad's old cross cut saw, which his forefathers had used to cut down mature timber before chainsaws were invented, and stole out to where the sign was. Jimmy's strong frame and my work hardened muscles made short work of the three 6 inch poles. As we sawed through the last one we exultingly pushed the whole hated towering mess over. It fell with a great crash and with the sound of police sirens. We were busted and spent the night in jail. I had already been to the cop shop several times but this time I went with my head held high for what I considered a worthy exploit! You may guess that my household never talked about the golden rule or the ten commandments.

One of my first teams; I am #21 Very sad because we just lost the championship game.

Chapter 3 For the Love of the Game

I began hardball at age 6. Baseball in a logging town in 1969 where kids fought almost every day in school looked like a whole different sport to the soft "its only a game" T-ball stuff they start kids out on now.   We played full on hardball where you had to hit a pitched ball and then you could steal when you made it to first.   By age 6 the toughest kids from Hungry Horse, Martin City and Coram gathered at a dirty little field by the train tracks in Coram, Montana, and super arms like Mike White and Bob Lietz hurled us fast horizontal pitches. There was none of this "it's only a game" stuff we were in it to win it, constantly used obnoxious banter to intimidate our opponent, and apart from being a good sport and shaking the other teams hand at games end it was war, comradery and high stakes bragging rights from the start.

For game jersey's we were encouraged to each buy a permanent marker and write our name and number on a white t-shirt. Coach quickly discovered I was a good hitter and since I was the fastest first grader in the three school region he really wanted me on the starting team. But he had a terrible time trying to find a defensive position for me. Tracing long fly balls in the outfield didn't come naturally for me and we had better infielders than I was.   Finally the industrious coach, Mr. Lakes, found this big pillow of a catchers mitt and stuck me behind the plate. If the ball came even close to the mitt it would get lodged in it! After an inning I told coach, "I like it; its gonna work!" From that moment on I was the undisputed catcher for the Canyon team.

This picture (page 11) was one of my first years playing and little Mike White also raced motocross and had arms like steel and though he was small could really crank some speed. Bob Lietz far right on bottom had a sidearm pitch that seemed to almost curve from the beginning. Kids who weren't warriors quit after a couple practices so we fielded pretty tough teams. That year I think we were sponsored by "Canyon Logging". The kids we played against from Columbia Falls were sponsored by industrial giants like The Anaconda Aluminum Plant or "Plum Creek." We'd arrive at their fancy ball diamonds and at first be in awe at their professional looking outfits and pitchers who could throw curve balls. But once we put our rally hats on and started screaming our "pitcher's got a rubber arm" or "we want a pitcher not a belly itcher" at them we would often end up with the win. My blood brother Jimmy, in front of coach was a helluva clean up hitter and I was blasting it out there well enough to receive talk that I might go really far with it someday. That year we worked our way through the brackets at the league end tourney till we ended up in the championship ! As a mouthy catcher I was a natural emotional leader so when we lost the close final game and posed for the team picture afterward you can see the look of extreme disappointment that I couldn't get off my face even for the team picture ! (I am number 21upper row far right.)

As ten year olds we were sponsored by the Husky Truck Stop in Coram and got an actual "Husky" patch to sew onto our white T shirts ! We fielded a tough squad again. This newspaper article says we "played a spectacular 14-1 season". We were really the team to beat in the year end tournament but once again fell short this time to my friend Mark Andersons' (Porter) team in the final. Interesting that just today as I am doing this edit Mark out of the blue posted this article about it on Facebook last night ;

Mark Porter is with **James West Willows**.

Yesterday at 7:00 PM · 👥

Glacier Twins of Columbia Falls lead by Mark Anderson (my real name was Porter but everyone called me Anderson because that was my step dads name). Defeat the pesky Huskies of Martin City/ Coram/ Hungry Horse lead by the mighty Buddy Willows! 1973!

👍❤️ 14   4 Comments 1 Share

HUSKIES OF MARTIN CITY-CORAM-HUNGRY HORSE played a spectacular 14-1 season, and were runners-up at Monday Little League tournament championship. From left front: Jim Short, Deelynn Olson, Buddy Willows, Bobby Lietz, Jimmy Hammons, Lewis Church, Darren Overcast; (back row) Tom Church, coach; Winfield West, Jody Kuzmic, Mike Potter, Johnny Johnson, Deven Walter, Ricky Allen, Tony Robinson, Jack Johnson, coach. Kevin and Colin Vaughn were absent.   Mel Ruder photos.

Baseball was going great except always being one of the best teams and placing second in the tourney. Second sucked ! So I kept pressing on for the prize of being the best.

My Dad was not a baseball player so I fueled my own fire watching my hero Johny Bench and his sidekick Pete Rose of the Cincinnati Reds wreak havok to their opponents. Then I saved my money from work and bought a back yard net that threw the pitch back to me. I practiced almost daily and really amazed crowds with the way I could snag batter pop ups behind the plate and even way over by the dugouts.

Home life was hectic to say the least and it gave me a sense of peace to excel at something. As a high energy athletic guy it seemed like as long as I was sore each spring from practices and staying focused on my sport I was also staying out of trouble for the most part. In 11 year old Pee Wee I played for Bob Cheff, a heck of a good coach then in 12 year old Pee Wee Harry Cheff and Dave Cotner coached us and we were proud to finally have real uniforms ! By then the league kept stats and I always liked to get up to the plate as clean up batter and have my, I think it was 400., batting average announced! I know it was the second highest average I ever heard come over the loudspeakers. (I heard a guy named Jay McClanahan, whom I later played with on All Stars, have a better one.) I was starting to notice and be noticed by some of the cute girls who worked the concession stand too and I sure didn't mind that ! Amazingly enough I still play for a Cheff at age 57 , Jake Cheff.

12 year old Pee Wee. I am the catcher on the far left. The guy next to me is Bob. He and I made all stars that year.

Today's kids are so civilized. No "hey batter batter -- SWING!" In contrast our squads were encouraged by our coaches to make plenty of noise and it was often the noisiest team that won close games. I was the Moham- med Ali of Canyon Baseball. I used my motor mouth to joke, distract, and bully our team to victory. Many a bat- ter got a little rattled when as the pitcher was winding up Buddy would tell 'em "yer shoe's untied !" That wasn't a good way to make friends with the opposing team and I paid for it dearly when studs from the other squads laid me out as I tried to block the plate as they came sliding in to home. I laid a few of them out too though and wasn't a bit afraid of the inevitable crashes at home plate ! Being a catcher is no place for a scared-e-cat and I gave it my all then and give it my all now too. I even got ejected from my softball game recently when I showed a little fire at the plate after we got a guy out with a beautiful line drive throw from our left feilder Cary Finburg and the ump called him safe. I threw my mit down on the plate and said, "He was fricken OUT !!!" "Catcher is ejected from the game the ump bellowed!" My team mates thought it was funny and I was just real glad I used an i not a u in my wording since they know I am a Christian and even a pastor.

Again we took dad gum second but had a great season. Other good pitchers Deelynn Olson and Jim Short came on strong and since I had signals with the pitchers for years we had it really going on by age 12 ! At the end of the season coach Harry and Dave said Buddy you and Bob have been voted by the players onto the All Stars. I normally worked summers so I had to ask for time off from my Dad who gave it to me but I had to ride my ten speed bicycle to all the practices because Dad was busy with the same kind of summer business I ran.

Once in All-Stars my big mouth got placed under wraps because the coach was also a highway patrolman and he told me to cool my jets.... but not my other jets; because I had good speed and quick reflexes I stole a lot of bases and usually won when I got in the hot box and this coach liked that. (Other coaches didn't like that about me and wanted the sure thing, don't risk it, get the run... I understand that but pushing the envelope gets runs too rather than leaving men on base at innings end.)

I knew I was probably the best catcher in the league especially when it came to stopping wild pitches and snagging pop ups but All-Stars to me was a dream I didn't totally expect come true! I had a natural home run swing and my 30 inch Louisville Slugger metal bat was one of the most solid metal bats I've ever swung--it seemed to be thicker gauge metal than today's bats. The combination made me a clean up hitter to contend with. I was peaking right during summer all stars

17

and often hit the most home runs in practice. One day I remember hitting three off the pitching machine in one at-bat. I was ready so we headed up to Pincher Creek, B.C., Canada. Bob and I put a sleeping bag in the tool box of Don Lietz's logging pick-up and had fun goofing around all the way to Canada. Coming from a real small town made the fancy ball diamonds and classy teams seem pretty cool. There was big talk about substantial prizes being handed out for individual player accomplishments. One of my first at-bats I slammed a fastball over the right center fence. My team-mates got me all excited because after I ran into the dug-out they told me they thought I'd win the biggest prize of all for the tourney's first home-run and they said it would be a boom box! Later that game my best buddy Bob caught an amazingly hard line drive to first. After the game we were on top of the world because Bob's catch earned him best play of the day and he got a free bucket of KFC chicken and my homer earned me a good prize. I don't remember what it was but was let down as it was NOT a boom box. Bob and I plumped out on chicken then went golfing for the first time. My experience was that hitting might get you there but pitching wins the big games. (Kind of like the NFL where offense may get you to the playoffs but defense wins the championships.) We had two big fast throwing pitchers; Tom Ladenburg, one of Columbia Falls' all time great athletes, and Chuck Higson; who played college ball then was recruited by the New York Mets. Not to mention Chris Dereu whose curve ball made Pamela Anderson look flat. Ron Pike was also solid and my friend Bobby's side-arm pitch stung my catcher's hand plenty. Our pitching depth left us looking solid against a physically huge team from Lethbridge, AB. and If I remember correctly we won the tourney! Or took second.

That was a nice trophy but when I became a Christian I threw it, my Punt, Pass, and Kick trophies, and my skiing trophies away because I thought they represented pride and vanity. Looking back I think I over-reacted as I would have liked to show my boys some of my trophies.

Next big tourney a fast bull jumped off the plate and caught me right in the adams apple. It shut me up and without my vocals urging us on we only got third but that was a really fun summer.

Chuck went to the Mets but I also caught some for an older kid named Randy Buzzel who threw much harder than Chuck. We all called him "Buzz" 'cause his pitches had a whizzing sound and stung my catching hand really bad if I didn't catch it in the pocket. His Dad wanted him to join the logging outfit so he never pursued baseball but many think he should have and he regretted not playing more ball.

A really high ball popped up in a practice game next spring I went charging out to get it. The third baseman, Jay Stratton, also went for it with gusto and we collided with a bang. I had to be benched and after 40 minutes in the dugout people insisted I get my big blue and purple left thumb checked out and when I did I found it was broken. It was set and put in a cast and it ended 13 year old ball. I wanted to hike the mountains real bad the next year so I didn't go out for 8th grade ball. I went out as a Freshman but by then we were grouped in with the upper-classmen and the field had gotten bigger. Almost no freshmen made the cut and I knew my frosh arm couldn't cut it at catcher so I didn't even keep coming to practice since I was more interested in chasin' girls and drinkin' beer by then and frittered away my high-school years.

On a construction site later in life I ran into one of my old coaches, and he said, "funny meetin' you here I always thought you'd end up playin' baseball on TV not swingin' a hammer!" That was a nice compliment and had my batting continued as it was some inventive coach may have found a position for me. (I'm not sure I had a good enough arm for a high level catcher--those dudes have to have a rifle-- but maybe I could have learned a better throwing technique or learned another position.) When a guy like me hits well over 300 with plenty of home runs coaches can usually find a place to stick you on the line up ! That coach wasn't the only one who thought I might have gone far so it made me hate pot which was the main derailer of my dream.

As a 47 year old I went out for baseball in the Division 3 college I attended in Texas. (Concordia Tornadoes) I did well enough to earn the respect of the entire team but did not earn a starting position.

After a 34 year break I really didn't have the timing to hit 87 MPH balls with proficiency but I did hit a few, make some friends and begin to learn a position other than catcher. My uncle Tommy Willows played baseball into middle age.

Now 57 I still play on a competitive softball team called the Wolverines. (third guy from right) As long as I play ball I stay in shape and stay out of trouble !

Ch. 4   Liking 7th Grade

I went from being a big fish in a class of about 15 kids in Hungry Horse to being plunged into Columbia Falls Junior High. (About 350 kids) Being the son of a Valedictorian had its perks; I always scored very high in the "Iowa Basic Test"... one year I scored in the top 1% of the nation. So I was always in the smartest kids class. In 7th grade that would be Mr. Wick (Homeroom) I was

known for Baseball and a lot of girls thought I was cute. I was girl crazy since the time I was 7 so going into the big school as a cute baseball star was like a dream come true. I enjoyed awkward note writing semi relationships with a few cuties but the day came when the girl many considered the cutest blonde in the school, I will call her Emma worked up the nerve to have her best friend call me; "Buddy, this is Carolyn ....Emma is in the room with me and she just wants to let you know she thinks you are cute !" I think she is really cute too Carolyn! Can I talk to her?" Emma was so shy she would rarely say more than "Hi" but I didn't care, a girl that cute didn't need to know how to talk as far as I was concerned! I invited her to the only movie theatre in town where all the kids made out. I was so nervous that I told myself "I will count to 100 and at 100 I will put my arm around her." I would get to 100 and then chicken out and start counting again. Finally after I had counted to 100 about three times I put my arm around her. I hadn't perfected

the "slide" technique so she thought someone from behind her was tapping her and she turned around kind-of
startled. I about freaked ! But she realized it was me and
settled in to snuggle.   We sure didn't care what show
was on as pretty soon we were making out real hot.   Did I
die and go to heaven? I thought maybe I did because she
was the cutest little blonde doll you ever did see!   My trip
to the afterworld ended abruptly after the movie because
when I walked to Dan's to spend the night afterwards I felt
2 large painful growths growing just under my ears. I got
"The Mumps" that night. Could a God I didn't believe in be
giving me a little sign that this wasn't the best path for
me? I don't know but an hour before I got herpes one
night my car got stuck out in front of the "Dew Drop Inn"
and I had to get 3 guys to help push me out before I took
home a hottie that was full of crabs and herpes! .... I later
wondered if God was trying to spare me some problems
that night too.   In all honesty I have greatly enjoyed every
girl I was ever overly friendly with but somehow I think I
missed God's best and opened an addictive avenue that
would sabotage my marriage later in life.   The kissing was
so good that for many weeks I didn't care if Emma had to
communicate with me through her best friend Carolyn.
But after awhile I also wanted a girl who could talk. So I
walked Emma out to the bus and before getting on, I said,
"I don't think this is working out baby, we just can't seem
to talk."   She continued till graduation to be a friend and
one of the WildCats hottest cheerleaders.   Since my Dad
was a good basketball player he almost forced me to live
out his dream at a sport I had little aptitude for but Emma
cheering on the sidelines kept the sorry second stringer
scoring about 4 points a game!   I was better at football
and had been our sixth grade quarterback and I had won
our areas "Punt, Pass and Kick" competition.

But after a few 7th grade football practices where they were trying me at running back my Dad told me, "Bud, you might break something doing that, come to work with me after school and I will give you $5.00 an hour" I wanted my own pick up so I did. The summer after 7th Grade I drank and partied the summer away with my older friend Jay who had a car. We often stayed out till 3 AM before sleeping out under the stars on my lawn. But up till then I was still a clean cut kid..... who was getting a reputation as a teenage alcoholic.

My 8th grade year (above) was a quality year for me because I had wholesome friends who were good influences. In the pic above is sister Jamey. Willow Dean below me. And my Father at a time of his life when we were living with a paralyzed mother and he was living in a little section of his business. He was a courageous, fun loving man but I think you could see in his face that it was a stressful season of his life just doing his duty. (next pic is of Dad, His Brother Jack who raised him and I)

Chapter 5 The Ivy League 8th Grader

The friends we find ourselves with shape us far more than we realize. Whenever someone told me about peer pressure I brushed it off because I often felt like I was the one leading or co-leading the relationships in my world. That may have been partly true but in retrospect I see that who I was close with shaped my world to a radical degree. In 8th grade the home room for the smart kids was Mr. Anderson's room and I made friends with a great guy in our class named Hugh Jones. Instead of drinking Hugh and I studied together, climbed mountains, and played basketball. He was good for me and I got on the high honor role every semester that year. At this point in my life I was the guy many parents would want their daughter to date; handsome, clean cut, industrious, great grades, and a second string player on the Columbia Falls Wildcats at my worst sport; basketball. (Dad insisting I'd be the next Jerry West at basketball made me vow to watch to find what my kids excelled in and promote that instead.)

Following my very successful 8th grade in school movies like "Grease", "Star Wars" and "Saturday Night Fever" punctuated a summer where I found myself drinking way too much and loving it. By the end of that summer I was living a dual life; like Dr Jekyl turning into Mr. Hide at full moon the mild partying smart jock would turn into a crazy party animal after about 10 beers or some Black Velvet. Being a naturally energetic person didn't help because my strong constitution propelled me to keep

24

going in that stupor till 3 or 4 in the morning. I'd come roaring into the trailer houses of some of my friends at 2:00 AM and say "Come on let's party! the night is still young!" I found myself partying till 4:00 AM most nights then getting up to work construction at 8:30 AM. I always had a good work ethic and didn't miss work. But by summer's end, after living above 100 m.p.h. with my fast driving mate Jay and drinking enough beer to drown an Elephant, I was a somewhat changed guy. I found landing that plane into the routine of school and tests and socializing with the right people was a rough landing at best.

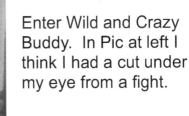

Enter Wild and Crazy Buddy. In Pic at left I think I had a cut under my eye from a fight.

As I entered high school some of the things that kept me sane... things like baseball, and academic motivation subsided. I continued to be a very successful cross country ski racer until I broke my leg badly at age 16, but that was the only wholesome activity that gave my energetic personality a good track to run on. My good friend Hugh really wanted to do all he could do to fit in with our schools highest clique of jocks. My growing hair and excessive partying habits didn't make me a prime candidate for that group and I said in my heart, "I think all these cliques are phony and mean so I am just going to be friends with everybody." Also in 8th grade I had a girlfriend that got good grades and was on the cross country ski team with me and she was a good influence. But I broke up with her my freshman year because I didn't like her jawline profile. I know it sounds so vain but I prefer a sculpted jawline like my x wife Jaekyung had.   These decent relationships were like tether lines keeping an over-inflated party blimp from floating off into the sky. Some people have a spiritual tether line but I had always been taught I evolved from apes so my logical conclusion from that ideology is that "if it feels good do it."   As I made this social migration I didn't realize it at the time but many good kids didn't want to be friends with a party animal. By then I was becoming well known for all the wrong things. I even pulled up to a girls house for Scotty to pick her up as a date and when the father found out I was in the car he wouldn't let the girl out of the house even though I was not her date! (He was a smart Dad) It wasn't all my fault that I was so wild. My sister Jamey, who was two years older, and I lived with a paralyzed mother who could not supervise us at all so much of our craziness was compounded by no boundaries and very little parental involvement. Relationships are of God. The reason the enemy attacks relationships so much is that proper relationships to family, friends, and fellow Christians keep darkness out of our lives and keep good things in.

The result of our home-life imploding is that Jamey and I were both at every keggar and both in many serious car wrecks. (In Montana there is often not much to do on the weekend so our habit was to get a 15 gallon aluminum keg of beer and build a big fire out in the woods and drink.) Since many of the good kids started kind of avoiding me I ended up hanging out with more and more stoners. Add daily pot and hash smoking to my L.S.D and Black-Velvet whiskey soaked weekends and I became a crazy party animal who now used his smarts and athleticism to perform crazy stunts like jumping off bridges onto railroad cars and hooky bobbing behind cars in winter and most of all racing. In the winter in Montana the roads get icy and slick so us guys would run up behind moving cars, in a sneaky way that the driver didn't detect, and grab their bumper and hang on without them seeing us as we slid behind....if you grabbed the right bumper in the right conditions you could achieve speeds of over 40 m.p.h.! Being brawny and catlike at diversions like "hooky bobbing" made me consider being a stunt man but for now I was the guy with the "I do all my own stunts" T-shirt! I bought a bright green 1970 Dodge pickup, put a genuine "Holley" carburetor on the 318 and won a few 1/4 mile races at the Lower Dam road in Hungry Horse! But my need for speed was about to go to a whole new level when my kind crippled Mom bought me the Little Green Buger ! :

Chapter 7   The Little Green Buger

Scotty was my best friend at the time and we had heaps of fun together. He had played baseball with me but now he was mainly interested in partying and girls so we became like Butch Cassidy and the Sundance Kid.   One night we got so drunk and took his dirt bike on a cruise through the ditch toward Hungry Horse. The bike began to weave and bob under the heavy influence of a smashed driver then BAM! We hit the rocky dirt hard. But we were so loose it didn't even hurt and we would laugh and laugh then remount only only to wreck again multiple times! Each time we would howl with laughter and jump back on for more.   That night I remember sleeping in Scott's Dad's queen size bed together and we just roared in laughter for a couple hours over anything and everything.... when you are really drunk it doesn't take much to get you laughing. (Us Montana guys often slept over in the same bed but we were all so girl crazy that we never had any other thoughts.... not very politically correct but it would not have been very safe to be gay in Montana at that time as guys like us thought that worthy of a black eye... not advocating that just sayin' what our culture was like.)

My Irish friend Scotty wasn't very tall but was very wide. Like most of the Downing clan from Martin City, Montana he was deceptively strong. I remember setting my pool cue down for a minute in a North Fork bar long enough to watch a burly 220 pound logger challenge Scotty (about 145 pounds) to arm-wrestle. Well, back to pool, that guy didn't last long either, Scott took him down quick. (After awhile it became a good side income for he and his cousin Mike because they stopped turning arms for free. I watched Mike win his weight division in a legit competition at the Log Cabin Bar and then work his way up the weight divisions till he had beaten even the burly heavyweight champion.) A few more rounds of "Oly" from the tap, a little flirting between pool games, and it was time to re-enter the "Little Green Buger" and blast off into the night.

The "Little Green Buger" was our outlaw bat-mobile. When I was 16 my loving Mom bought a Mercury Capri from the deacon at her church. I was elated when I looked at the dash for the first time and saw that the speedometer went to 160 miles per hour. What a nice present but a car with a speedometer that goes to 160 mph. isn't exactly the smartest present to give your party animal 16 year old. The car was the ugliest green color ever conceived. The little Mercury was really just a long front end full of 6 cylinders of high compression horsepower! The cramped cockpit barely held Scotty and I and anybody crazy enough to get into the cramped back seat.

The Deacon had put a sticker that said "I Found It" on the back bumper. In that era that slogan meant that the owner had been "born-again" and found God. Instead of taking the sticker off Scott and I found a sticker for our favorite kind of pot, "Kona Gold." We put that on so it read, "I Found It; Kona Gold!" The car was the pukiest shade of citrus green Detroit ever devised.

29

One day Jim Short or someone exclaimed "Buddy your ugly car looks like a "little green buger!" It was meant to be an insult but our twisted minds liked it and our ride officially became "The Little Green Buger!' Only goofy dudes like us could ever take pride in such a name but we did; we got some chrome tape and carefully cut out the name which we proudly displayed in the back window.

I had a reputation as a crazy but steady driver. Scott liked to brag about the night even "Snortin' George" insisted on getting out. It was the night of the homecoming football game. I was preparing to be one of Jay Winters' best men and had rented a beautiful white tux with flowery green breast ruffles. One of my old girlfriends from my "good jock" days was in the running for homecoming queen so she wanted me to be her escort out onto the football field at half time. So I wore the tux but I also wore my "Stetson" partying hat over my shoulder length hair! It was a big hit with my classmates that night! After the homecoming football game there was a big keggar in the woods. We'd dropped some good acid in addition to our usual assortment of beer, Black-Velvet Whiskey, Tequilla, and Pot. The combination made me a little edgier than my normal speedy self. As Scotty and I were leaving Snortin' George asked to ride into town with us. You can probably guess how he got his name "Snortin' George," and he had a reputation as a crazy driver himself. Knowing I had a driver of some renown in my back seat I didn't want the ride to town to be boring so I went through the gears going from 0 to 90 on the gravel road in a flash then I dropped it into third and clutched out just enough to grab that perfect edge where the car does a controlled power slide around the corner. I thought I was putting on an impressive display but as my car came out of the gravel corner, still going fast, Snortin' George leaned up, slammed his hands onto the back of the seat and demanded, "let me out right now, I'm walkin'!!" We got a big kick out of it and teased him as a wussy for a bit but when we realized he was dead serious I stopped and let him out. Reflecting back on the incident I would have saved myself a broken leg and other scares if I had been as smart as George was that night but Scotty got a big kick out of how my driving had scared even Snortin' George and retold the story at many a keggar!

The Little Green Buger had some great accessories. It came equipped with a sunroof that would crank back all the way. I would crank it back then drive with my knees so that Scott and I would both be sticking out of the car from the waist up. We could wave, call out to girls, throw snowballs, or just let our long hair blow in the breeze but we thought it was pretty rad.

The high grade stereo with additional amp really made Eric Clapton, Van Halen, and Molly Hatchet sound great and the tiny back seat sported a little custom art my friend Wendy Guiterez put there with her red lipstick..... she wrote, "Rose Hips was here." My girl Sam and I fogged up the windows a time or two but "Rose Hips" was a fictitious character. I thought it was cool though and it went well with my Playboy air refresher which hung from the rear view mirror. Since "The Little Green Buger" is a prop in this play I thought you, the reader, should get acquainted with the car which all the cops certainly became acquainted with.

If I was a cop in that era I would have stopped "the Little Green Buger" even if it was parked because there was always something illegal taking place there. One time a sheriff did stop by even though we were parked. Dave Finch and I had lots of beer and whiskey in the car and we were both under age so when the imposing "Pig", is what we called the law, stepped up to my window and said, "What's going on here?!" I said, "my car died and just won't start." The officer kindly helped us open the hood and shined his flashlight on things: "Now try it," he said. The Little Green Buger was equipped with a toggle switch under the dash that would turn the car completely off so I flipped the switch to off and cranked it over awhile. Seeing the car wouldn't start we asked him to help push us so we could coast down the big hill into down town Hungry Horse. He agreed so we all pushed it then we coasted down the hill coming from the Hungry Horse Dam. Dave and I cracked up laughing so hard at how we'd fooled him! He must have been watching us roar because a half a minute later his lights were on be-hind us and as we reached the "Log Cabin Bar" he ran up to my car and practically tore me out of it while he un-covered my fifth of whiskey and 12 pack of beer in the back seat. We got another free ride to the Columbia Falls jail for under-age drinking that night. That night they told me, " Buddy Willows you are getting quite a record and if we so much as catch you doing ANYTHING illegal again we will send you to Pine Hills (boys prison) for six months! I was already on parole for other incidents.

My high school years in the Little Green Buger and in my friends muscle cars were often like a scene from "The Fast and the Furious" series! Here are a few of the more memorable races and wrecks I was in;

Chapter 8   A Few Memorable Car Races and Wrecks

My Dad had grown up with no father present so he was pretty independent and felt I should be the same. So at age 12 he said I could have his old Volkswagen pick-up. (Like a Volkswagen hippie bus with it's rear end made into a pick-up.) But Dad told me I could only drive it on the back roads. Before a ball game my pitcher Bob and I were driving around listening to The Eagles. I told him, "Bob grab the wheel for a bit while I change the cassette." ii had a portable deck wired in to my speakers and looked down to change the music. All of a sudden WHAM! and when I looked up there was a huge birch tree that we had hit dead center! It had smashed through the bumper and pushed the middle of the truck in at least a foot! I had smashed out the front window with my head! "Bob you OK?" I asked. "ya I think so." "Why didn't you steer like I asked you to?" Bob replied "Steer? I never heard you ask me to steer!" First rule of communication make sure the other person heard what you said! :)

If you head up the "North Fork Road" about 4 miles outside of Columbia Falls you will come to a straight stretch of road with plenty of burn out marks on it. This is where we raced either 1/4 mile or 1/2 mile races. This particular day I was in Jay's gold Lemans and we were driving right over the center line at about 100 m.p.h. and the other car was driving right at us over the center line at a similar speed. The game was called "chicken." The first car who chickens out and veers from the head on course is the loser. The distance closes really fast at a combined speed of around 200 m.p.h.! My Val Kilmer cool was starting to shake...

My car today 71 Camaro SS with numbers matching 350 built to 520 horsepower

I liked the wheel in my own hand at times like this but I trusted Jay implicitly as we lived above 100 m.p.h.. At the last possible moment the other car veered as we did also! Wheeww....>>> playing games like this got the adrenaline pumping! You may surmise that we got in a few wrecks and we certainly did. But far fewer than we should have partly because we were damn good drivers.

Deer hunting with plenty of beer 60 miles west of Great Falls, Montana with my good buddy Jay was always great. We were not the best hunters but driving around drinkin' beer and listening to music always enabled us to catch a buzz if nothing else. Today we had gone out with some of his cousins from Great Falls. His cousin Jamey in the black Ford step-side wanted to race me back to town so we agreed the loser would have to buy the other a six pack and floored it! I was about 16 at the time and drove my full size 1970 Dodge pickup which had a 318, Holley carb., and 4 speed. Nothing to brag about but I was crazy enough to make it go pretty good. For the most part we just drove 90 - 100 m.p.h. while passing people and hugging the curves pretty tight. But I was intensely competitive and when I could see he was going to beat me I did something drastic! I watched the string of cars coming in the oncoming traffic lane and knew I really couldn't pass him. Meanwhile my rival Jamey couldn't pass either because he was behind some law abiding citizen. It was then I took to the right shoulder. It was a fairly wide eastern Montana style right shoulder with room enough between the white line and the reflectors so I floored it and went flying by numerous cars and was about to pass Jamey's step side Ford pickup too.....I thought I had stretched my luck a little too far though because I saw a strong guard rail approaching where the hiway crossed some water.....   I about s--- my pants however when I saw the guard rail approaching fast because it cut off my lane!   pg. 34

Jay and I both knew it would be tight if I got the last car passed before slamming into the guard rail. Jay exclaimed "Buddy you crazy son of ....." It was truly a moment of decision. Either I abandon the folly, hit my brakes and lessen the impact or else I floor it." I floored it and my speedometer soared and my 16 inch 6 ply work tires held fast against the part gravel part pavement floor. Jamey to the left of me was pretty miffed but couldn't really keep up as I powered up from the right shoulder and narrowly missed the stalwart galvanized guard rail. At that second I realized I was really stupid but also realized the people behind me would get my license plate if I didn't scoot so I floored it with the mixed emotion of endangering people and of exulting in my apparent victory over Jamey. I crossed the bridge into town first but he then took some local boy short cut to supposedly beat me to the "Entering Great Falls" sign. I was pissed that he wanted me to buy the beer. Thank God most kids today can get their kicks through video games instead of through the real thing like we did! The only video game we had was pong and it didn't hold a candle to this!

That was one of the few times Jay was the passenger. He was 2 years older than I so I was usually the one holding my breath during his crazy exploits. He and I were like "The Dukes of Hazard" though because we drove fast and crazy so often that it began to seem almost normal. Jay was an amazingly good driver and even though speeds well in excess of 120 were not unusual for us I always felt pretty good with him at the wheel. He should have been in NASCAR. He sported a sweet gold Pontiac Lemans with a fairly new 350 race edition engine in it.

A few cars beat him in the quarter mile but no one could touch us when it came to top end speed. I don't know that we ever really did see how fast she could go but one night I remember us going over 150 on that straight stretch right in front of "The House of Mystery" on U.S. Hwy. 2.

Most Saturday nights the muscle cars would take to cruising main in Kalispell where we would usually either pick up a chick, a race, a fight, or a hangover. The lights provided a good "Christmas Tree" to signal the start of block long races and at the end of "the strip" was the Rosaurs parking lot where we would turn around and create mischief. We were tough, proud, and knew we were fast so when the driver of a green Nova flipped us off as they exited the Rosaurs parking lot the chase began. We screeched after them right on their tail going past "Wood-Land Park." As we came to that stop before entering U.S. 2 I extended my whole upper body out of the passenger side window and plastered the back of the Nova with beer bottles. My aim was on and I watched in glee as they shattered against the Nova's back window. We were fast but so was the Nova! They outgunned us down a stretch of highway then turned onto some obscure gravel road I had never been on. As the Nova's headlights zipped down the gravel road at well over a hundred we kind of shook our heads at each other as we realized how fast the car was, maybe even faster than we were! But what we lacked in horsepower we made up with by being a little crazier and having a steady hand at the wheel. We gained on them. Then to our utter horror the unthinkable happened; the Nova's tail lights turned to the right then disappeared. We knew that could mean only one thing, they had taken an L turn 100 feet in front of us. At that time we were probably going about 80 m.p.h. and slowed ourself to maybe 45 by the time we were entirely inside the gravel L turn. I saw my life flash in front of my eyes as the Lemans slid fast off the road. It was like in slow motion and the slide seemed to take forever. I remember trying to brace myself for the inevitable roll over I knew we would be taking. I had never been in a car that rolled but I had often thought what I would do if it happened so I braced myself well. As our rear tires went off the road and the momentum of the car started the roll there was a huge thud and shards of glass from the exploding driver side windows came toward us like a thousand tiny knives. To our amazement the car never rolled, instead we hit a huge post that held a farmers mailbox! The impact acted like a sling shot and shot us back onto the road. Was this a premonition of the way my out of control life would one day run into "The Rock of Ages" and be put back on a decent road? I sure didn't think about it at the time but our battered Lemans limped a few blocks down the road then we pulled over to view the damage. The whole side of Jay's car was caved in. Just then an old pickup with an angry farmer stopped on the road next to us. "Are you the boys who just took out my mail box!" He snorted. Jay replied, "No it was those guys up there!" as he pointed to the vanishing lights of the Nova. "Then why are you out there looking at the damage?" The farmer said. Jay replied, "we're just out here takin' a piss." The farmer roared after the Nova and we jumped in, turned a Ueee and somehow drove Jay's Lemans clear back to Hungry Horse. Jay's Dad Bill was a street smart trucker with a good sense of humor. The car was totaled and we agreed to tell his parents that someone hit us while we were parked when we were inside the movie theatre. His Dad Bill just grinned when we said it and replied, "ya and I am sure the person who hit you had a wooden bumper!"

(Because Bill had pulled a sliver of wood out of the wrecked door.)   Jay's Mom Shirley spent a day pulling glass shards out of Jay's face but other than that we were both OK!

The only "problem" with the Gold Lemans was that it was a four door (It was a powder puff of a sweet car inside and out but cool dudes prefer to cruise in a two door.) Jay bought an old green Lemans that needed a motor from a buddy for $250.00. (Jay always had money because he actually liked to work…we worked as carpenters together for my Dad and endured many a day of bad beer farts but never missed work.) We got busy with our wrenches and soon had the 350 race motor in the new rod.   The gold rod had high gears that maximized the great horsepower. The green one had low gears and all we could really do is go around burning rubber. It was like trading in a Benz for a beat up Corolla and we realized our glory days were kind of over. Still Mr. Winters let Jay use his slick black Chevy truck that held a 454 so we still had a few kicks.

In memory of the Gold Lemans I will tell one more story about it. Jay claims that a cop turned on his lights around the "Stop and Shop" leaving Columbia Falls. Jay knew he had the faster car so he just gunned it going up the North Fork where we used to race 1/4 and 1/2 mile races and have keggars. The cop flew after him but could not catch the Lemans which would easily go over 150 m.p.h.. The fuzz stayed in pursuit but Jay turned down the "Blankenship Bridge" road which is a gravel road that is famous for kicking up a plume of dust that could choke a Hippo. Jay knew that road like the back of his hand and ended up losing the cop by using the dust to his advantage.

Since Jay was alone I have no way of verifying the story but I believe him as he and I outran cops once or twice on our snowmobiles.

I was on the Columbia Falls High School Cross Country Ski team. I was doing very well and had won the last three races I was in. In one race I beat a seasoned Australian racer and he liked my spirit so much that he gave me his "Kongsberg" brand racing skiis which I was really excited about because I had been racing on old wooden race skis. My usual practice was to follow the lead racer the whole race then pass him in the end but with my fancy new skis I just zoomed out to first place and held that position till the end in the last race I was in. People were talking about me getting a college scholarship for skiing. (I still smoked pot but I laid off the partying some during ski season because to me it was a good rush to ski 10 kilometers in 30 minutes and I loved meeting the hot swedish girls who would show up at the races! Nothing quite as breathtaking as a Swedish blonde in perfect ski racing form.) But then disaster struck. Jimmy and I went to see a Clint Eastwood film called "Every Which Way But Loose" with one of our friends. After the movie the friend was driving too fast on treacherous black ice. (Where it had been raining then froze.) We asked him twice to slow down but we were a little stoned and it didn't seem to register. Then as we crossed the bridge heading east on what is now Montana Hwy. 35 coming out of Kalispell. His Ford pickup broke loose at about 60 m.p.h. on a curve. First the pickup went sliding down the highway sideways in the oncoming traffic lane. (It was a 2 lane Highway.) Had there been oncoming traffic we might all be dead but fortunately no one was coming. Then we fishtailed and found ourself going down our own lane sideways with the rear of the truck in the ditch. The rear tire caught on an incoming access farm road and when it did it thrust me with great force against the passenger door and I popped out going maybe 40 m.p.h.. I found myself in mid air about to hit the gravelly shoulder of the highway. Being from a baseball background I assumed the position I would have if I was sliding into second base after a steal. I took the nasty slide ok but then my right boot hit the oncoming reflector and I tumbled. During the tumble the reflector gashed open my back just behind my kidney. I might have been OK but a 200 pound piece of Tamarack firewood our friend had in the back of his Ford popped out upon impact also and came tumbling through the air and came down hard upon my left knee and thigh! I was in great shape from being a ski racer so I thought I would just dust myself off and go home. The first thought that came to me is that the police would surely come so I had better get rid of the pot and the pipe in my pocket. I stood up to throw it into the field and my left leg crumbled like "Jello." It turned out I had broken the largest bone in my body, the Femur, completely in half and I had also pulled my knee completely apart. The pain was intense and as I lay in the ambulance all I could think was, "this kind of stuff always happens to other people not to me." Some people were starting to breath the word "Olympics" in association with my racing. Whether that was realistic or not I don't know but I loved the sport enough to practice 2 or 3 hours a day. But now one thing was certain, My serious ski racing career was over. (I did come back to race even in events up to 50 Kilometers in my twenties but no longer as a serious national level contender.) I writhed in pain on the emergency room table until they cut my jeans off and gave me major injections of morphine. I instructed them, "those are brand new Levi 501's please cut them off carefully and save them for me." Even with the morphine the pain was unbearable and I asked if they had anything stronger for the pain. They just shook their sympathetic heads no. My father wisely secured a great surgeon for me named Dr. Hillebo who used awesome stainless steel pins and screws to put me back together. But still I lay in the hospital bed for what seemed like forever getting several quarts of blood a day at first. The doctor informed me that the growth plate inside my femur would seal shut at the total break and I would be lopsided as my other leg continued to grow. But my grandma took it to prayer her prayers helped the bone to heal up with inner marrow unhindered by a calcium wall! When I was 18 I did not get a lawyer and fight for it but I did receive a settlement for the injuries I sustained. The driver of the vehicle later accused me of jumping out just to get the insurance settlement. I told someone that and they said, "no one dumb enough to jump out of a truck in a out of control scenario would be smart enough to calculate doing so at that instant to get insurance money." I didn't "jump out" any more than the 200 pound piece of Larch firewood that broke my leg "jumped out" ! The reality is that when his right rear tire hit that oncoming farm access road, hard enough to bend the rim by the way, the impact caused both me and the Larch chunk to explode out. I didn't even know I would get a settlement from it till much much later when I turned 18. I certainly did not jump out and break my femur and end my racing career on purpose! (I forgive him and wish him the best and find it unfortunate he seems to believe that I jumped out as it kind of ruined our friendship.) I was in other memorable races and wrecks but these are ample tales to furnish you a feel for the fast and furious aspect of my life.

Me at a 50 K race I was in during my twenties. (I was no longer a national level racer at this point)

Many of the best racers were from Norway and Sweden. This Swede I raced against went on to the Olympics

I am number 427 in this large race!

Chapter 9   A Few Memorable Fights

My father's name was James Lake Willows. Everybody called him Jim. He was a smart likable guy with plenty of swag but you didn't want to get on his bad side because he wasn't afraid of anybody. One time when Dad was about 60, and had just come off an appendix surgery, the tough 35 year old logger from next door came over and in a gruff voice told Dad, "Willows you better keep that dog of yours the hell off my property!" Dad doubled up his giant hand and said, "Framness, I'll give you about 5 seconds to get off my property before I hit you so damn hard in the jaw you won't know what happened to ya!" He left!

Dad got in many fights around town but the most famous one became known as the "Hungry Horse Rock Festival." In those days in Hungry Horse there were no eviction notices for renters you just went and raised hell with them till they paid. Well Dad had this renter named Chuck whose 230 pounds fell solidly on his 6'3" frame. Dad needed his rent from him so the two began to feud. Chuck came down the hall of my Dad's restaurant into the little room where Dad lived and plunged through the door ready to jump on Dad. Dad took his old style typewriter and threw it at Chuck striking him in his almost bald head! This provided enough of a distraction for Dad to run out of the small room and across the street into the town park. A good fighter picks the place where the fight should take place if he can and the open space favored my agile father. Chuck ran after Dad but Dad kept a few paces ahead of him and would continually turn around and pelt Chuck with stones. It became famous because it was in the central park for all to see. Eventually Chuck got tired of the stoning and gave up. When I interviewed my Dad after the fight he said, "I knew if that giant ever got his hands on me I'd be done for so I just had to use the typewriter and the rocks to keep him at a distance!" One of my favorite spiritual and life principles is to find a way to win. Dad found a way to win that afternoon and the incident became known as "the famous Hungry Horse Rock Festival!" (It drew quite a crowd.)

Dad's second favorite story was when he came to school in sixth grade and the huge class bully was picking on people again. No one had ever challenged the dude before but Dad told him to quit it. This resulted in an after school fight. Dad said the fight went on for a long time with Dad just boxing him and keeping just out of reach of the hulk. After a few rounds the big kid wore down and Dad closed in with a well placed right cross to the nose and left hook to the solar plexus till the kid said he'd had enough. After that Dad was the hero of the class. He was very popular in school and became both the class president and the class valedictorian. Pretty good for a poor kid who lived with his Mom !

Dad's favorite fight story however was the day his Dad fought the man who would later go on to fight the heavyweight champion of the world. Dad's eyes would light up as he'd tell me the story for the fifteenth time;

A man named Bob Fittsimmons was doing what they called "barnstorming" through Lewiston, Idaho. His group offered $500.00 to anyone who could stay in the ring with Bob for 3 rounds. Back then a round was when one of the fighters got knocked down.

Buckskin Jimmy Willows

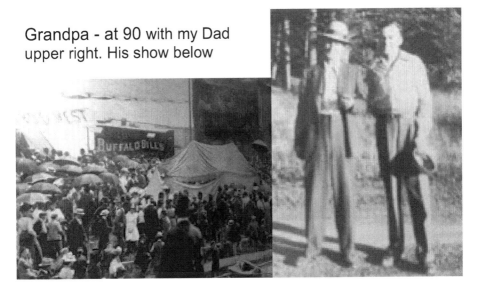

Grandpa - at 90 with my Dad upper right. His show below

Buckskin left home at 14, pretty common in 1870 and went to work for "Buffalo Bill" on his Kansas ranch and later Jimmy became part of the Wild West Show doing feats of strength.

Lewiston Idaho, 1896: As the announcer scanned the crowd for a taker people said, "get buckskin Jimmy Willows to fight him." Buckskin was Dad's father who was a well liked rancher that was known to be tough. Jimmy took him up on the offer. Buckskin stepped over the rope and strode across the dirt and sawdust floor of the ring to shake hands with his opponent before the bell. Now I know where Dad got his fearlessness because as Buckskin looked Fittsimmons in the eye it was not the look of a man ready to take a pounding but it was the look of a man who thought he might just give a pounding. They fought long and hard and Willows went down. Then to the crowds surprise a hard right from Willow's giant working man's hand (no gloves back then) found Fittsimmons' chin and the champ hit the sawdust hard. He shook his head and got up. I can't remember what happened next but I know that when the fight was over Buckskin Jimmy Willows not only won the $500.00 but Bob walked over to him and said, "Willows why don't you join me barnstorming, you'd make a helluva lot more money fighting than ranching!" Willows declined but from then on was a home-town hero in Idaho. I relished that story because the only way for Grandpa to not win is if he got knocked down and stayed down. That is like us in life; the circumstances of life will hit us hard sometimes but the only way to lose is if we don't get back up after going to the mat. The only real way for us to lose is to get knocked down and stay down ! Dad said Fittsimmons went on to fight James Corbett for the heavyweight championship of the world in Las Vegas a year or two later.

With legends like that in the glory days of my kin it was hard to grow up as a wimp. I remember the first time I came home from school with a black eye and complained to Dad about how a bigger kid blasted me in the face. He said, "well I guess it's time to teach you how to box." He filled up a faded green canvas bag with sawdust and hung it from a rope in the room that he stored his paint in. He proceeded to give me lessons on how to use my jab then come in for the right cross that could be followed with a left hook. I remember my wimpy arms and soft fists hitting that hard canvas bag for the first time. It scuffed my puny knuckles and it did not make me feel too confident. But eventually I'd go in and pound on it with some gusto and I soon became tied for the toughest kid in my class. When a new kid came to class he had to either fight Dan or me. (Not his real name.) Then he would have to race me because I was the fastest kid in the class. The Hungry Horse grade school was filled with kids who settled their differences with their fists. It was routine for kids to meet on the trail home and fight after school. And as they'd fight other fights usually broke out. One memorable day for me was the day I had three fights. First there was this new kid we called ski slope because his nose came sloping down like a ski jump. He was telling me how tough he was and was showing me these Judo moves he knew and I said something to him like, "do you think that would work in a real fight." He gave a cocky answer so I came at him with both fists blazing and him and his little Judo back flip caved in like a snow tunnel. As I was walking back to the playground Woody Winters shouted out his usual, "I'll kick yer butt BUDDY WILLLOWS!!!" No matter how many times I would whip him Woody was always sure he could take me. So Woody and I had our usual 60 second fight that ended with me on top. Then after school some other smart aleck mouthed off to me. I came after him and Dwight Lansing picked up a rock and threw it at me. I remember seeing it coming. It was a flat but solid skipping stone coming in with a curve. It curved just enough to avoid my arm which was trying to deflect it and it hit me perfectly in the balls. That really made me mad so I think it was him that was my third fight of the day.

I could beat up anyone in my class but Dan but it was kind of scary the day a big sixth grader sent me a note saying he wanted to fight me after school. I was a fifth grader and I remember looking across the room at him. I smiled real nice to him hoping he would take it easy on me. Since I had to protect my reputation I squared off in the narrow trail after school to face Jay Stratton. The snow was real deep on either side of the trail so after throwing a few punches his strong hands grabbed my coat then I knew it would be a wrestling match which I didn't like because he was bigger. It didn't take him long to somehow grab my head and plunge it into 18 inches of wet heavy snow. I remember the awful feeling of not being able to breathe so I had to quit. I hated to tap out but not being able to breath is scary! I remember that fight because it was one of the only ones I ever quit in.

A good way to win a fight is to just out endure your opponent! Because kids get tired in a fight and if you can outlast them you can usually win!

Dan and I were friends since before Kindergarten and we ruled the class together. We worked in tandem to create plenty of problems for our teachers. One day Dan and I had to both stay 1/2 hour after school for mischief. Mr. Mahugh left the room so I jumped on Dan's shoulders and changed the big black school clock to 3:45. When the teacher came back we informed him our time was up and he incredulously looked at the clock and let us go. We busted up laughing as soon as we left the building and Mr. Mahugh came running after us and put that iron grip of his around our cocky arms and dragged us back into the room! Even though we got caught we rejoiced in how we bested him! Being typical mean kids we also terrorized our classmates. One day Dan and I executed a carefully arranged plan; he poked the fat girl in class, she opened her whining mouth as far as it would go exclaiming, "Danny Osborn I'm gonna tell..." but right then I shot a spit wad through my straw precisely into her gap-

ing mouth! (large girl in center of back row in pic)   It was fun being the joint kings of the class. (I am in the back row on the left in the pic on the previous page. I had Rheumatic Fever that year so I stayed in the classroom at recess with the teacher I developed a crush on, Ms. Robertson.)

It was fairly normal for me to come home with a fat lip or a black eye but the brawl that far exceeded all the others was the day Dan and I fought. We often pushed, shoved, and wrestled dead even for 30 minutes at a time but since we were friends we never truly fought. This day after 4th or 5th grade was different. We decided to fight after school and the news spread like wildfire that the two kings were going to rumble! A big crowd gathered in the ponderosa pine forest East of the school. There is a certain nervous adrenaline rush before a good fight and I remember feeling a pretty good shot of it as I boxed toward Dan. He came in hard with his fists flying trying to overpower me. I kept him at bay with my jab and landed a cross but not before a couple of his windmill punches found their mark.   We kept this frenzy up for what must have been a full ten rounds. Toward the end we were so tired that we were almost falling back into "our corners". Then Stu Milco (we called him milk cow) would grab Dan and push him back toward me and Jimmy and others would keep me from falling and shove me back toward Dan.   The crowd was all saying it was the best fight ever but neither Dan nor I could really get the decisive advantage and we were both tired of bloody noses and fat lips so finally we just called it a draw, hugged each other and walked off friends! Back to ruling Hungry Horse grade school as the undisputed and equal champions of the class. Since we had no desire to fight each other again Dan and I conceived a plan to fight the toughest 6th grader which was our friend Jimmy Grant. Jimmy had a big chest and even as a 6th grader he threw hay bales in the summer so his biceps were swollen and by ourselves Jimmy would have beat the crap out of us but Dan and I decided we would challenge Jimmy to fight

both of us at the same time! To make it a real fight we would also get the equalizing advantage of having spears ! At this time Dan and I had both made some super sharp fire hardened wood spears that we tried to hunt stray dogs with. Jimmy agreed to fight us even with our spears! Again it was an after school event and a pretty good crowd gathered to watch. Jimmy roared after Dan to start with and jerked his spear right out of his hand and broke it over his knee. This gave me a great chance to get behind Jimmy, having the advantage I placed the sharp spear point right behind his lungs and started to apply pressure. I asked myself, "should I go ahead and run him through so we win?" I answered myself, "no if I do that who is going to be my good friend?.... besides if I so much as break his skin he will really pummel me."   Not having the guts to skewer him proved fatal because Jimmy was about done with Dan by then so he turned on me and pulled my head down and simultaneously brought his knee up hard into my solar plexus. Both Dan and I tried to fight on bravely but it was almost done before it started. Later we decided we would have done much bet-ter if we didn't have the stupid spears because neither of us had the guts to run Jimmy through anyway!

Guys Who Did Have the Guts to use their Weapons;

My Mom had a bad stroke when I was about 10 so in 6th grade I lived with a paralyzed mother who was loving but seriously impaired. Dad lived six blocks away and just came home to yell at us once a day and bathe Mom. My sister Jamey and I emptied Mom's bedpan at night, cooked TV dinners for ourself, and could stay out late partying which we often did.   The summer after sixth grade I started running with an older kid named Jay and his cousin Jimmy. We would drink, drive fast, and chase girls till the wee hours of the morning. One night we decided to go find some Indians to beat up at the South Fork Saloon in Martin City.   It was two poor Native Americans called the McCurdy brothers. Jay went in the bar to pick the fight and these guys were more than willing to oblige. So Jay waited in front of the bar and McCurdy came running out of the bar with a three foot pipe wielded above his head screaming his war cry all the while! Jay was a good school wrestler and had the advantage of fighting his three younger brothers every week.   So a screaming Indian with a pipe didn't rattle him much he just got inside the swing of the pipe, got McCurdy in a headlock with one arm and started pummeling him with the other fist.   Jay was a real good guy to have around in a fight. Some of my other friends may have been tougher than him but Jay was brave.... sometimes brave is better than tough when in the thick of things I found out the hard way.

That fight was good practice for Jay because a couple years later a big hunter named Joe, Jay, Danny Nicholas, and I were out cruising main in Kalispell at 1A.M. when we jealously noticed two guys in an Impala low rider that had some hot girls...we had got skunked in that department so far that night so we pulled up to their Impala. Joe was a great comic and a complete smart ass. When we drove up next to the Impala Joe rolled down the window and said to the guy driving, "How would you young

ladies like to get your ass kicked by some real men?!" I
was pretty drunk and in the back seat but I knew the fight
was on so I tightened up the laces on my logging boots
and practiced a few kicks as we awaited the "young ladies" in the parking lot of the Husky gas station. The
guys looked small in the lowrider but I gulped when they
got out of the car because they were about 6 foot 3 and
had long muscular arms. It was two against four but
these dudes were big! As big blondie approached our
biggest guy Joe he pulled out a torque wrench he had
concealed behind his thigh and with a long arcing swing
landed a powerful blow right on Joe's head. Joe went
down like a 200 pound sack of flour and the murderous
tough guy lunged at me next. I always ran with older
guys so I was just 15 with this 17 or 18 year old guy that
is way bigger in every way coming at me with a 21 inch
torque wrench poised above his head. I was ashamed of
my action but I put my forearm up to cover my head, and
said "I'm not in this" as I backed up. He shifted his focus
to Jay who did the same thing he did with the Indian,
quickly moved inside the swing of the pipe, grabbed onto
the guy and started swinging. Danny was able to take
the torque wrench away from him and the two had a
pretty good fight while chicken Willows watched.

I wasn't always a chicken though, one night a big guy
came up to Dan, Scott Downing and I at a party in Whitefish, MT. He said, "I'll take all three of you punks on." I
felt pretty bold that night and right behind the dude was a
sweet blonde I was trying to impress so I blurted out real
loud, "I'll take you on ALL BY MYSELF!!" He said, "I'll be
waitin' out front." I thought "Oh no what did I get myself
into now?!" I asked John Hanks, who was from Whitefish, "is that George guy

tough?" He said, "I don't know but you better get out there because he's waitin' for ya." To be honest it was with some fear and trepidation that I stepped out onto the large front porch to face this guy that outweighed me by about 30 pounds and was a couple years older. But I had a little false courage given by the shots of Black Velvet. As soon as I came out the door he came at me with a storm of flying fists. All I could really do is weave and duck and box back a little. Since he was so much bigger than me, I was really not able to go on the offensive. I just fielded another charge and was glad to see I was still on my feet. He backed up a little evidently pissed that I was still up. He cursed then came on strong again. I was pushed by his weight up against the house but I felt light on my feet compared to the big slugger. Nevertheless his charge almost pinned me up against the side of the house. Maybe I saw his left cross coming and his teeth clenched or maybe it was just my fast reflexes. But I ducked at just the right split second and the next thing I remember is the sound of crashing glass and screaming girls. I had ducked under his hard punch and his left arm went right through the large plate glass thermal pane window which was behind me. The sharp glass had laid his arm open pretty good in several places and blood was squirting out. Amidst the sounds of the screaming girls I heard somebody say, "call the ambulance!" I was really kind of glad it was over so I found my buddies who were all patting me on the back and I was really kind of the hero of the party that night. I was hoping Jo-anne the freshman blonde I'd been trying to impress would come congratulate me but maybe she didn't like fights because to my displeasure she had left the party. Funny how as a teenage guy you think you are going to get the girl by having a big impressive fight when really all they wanted was for you to come grab their hand and snuggle with them in the corner sofa! Pretty soon the Ambulance came and got George and the night faded into another hangover. Next week at school some guys had heard about it and I thought I was pretty cool, I jokingly bragged to Jim Short, "These hands put a man in the hospital last week!, they should be registered with the government as lethal weapons!"

That was probably the pinnacle of my fighting career although I entered the boxing smoker between Whitefish High and Columbia Falls High and did pretty good and that time the girls WERE impressed! I remember getting knocked out in a sparring match in preparation for the smoker. That was a weird feeling, my eyes saw black, I went blank for a bit and then my ears were ringing. I was thankful for my buddy Don Hanks giving me a lesson to prepare me for the smoker. His brother went pro and Donny was almost as good. (So sad to hear the friend I boxed in the smoker died in a logging accident.)

In grade school we kids would duke it out full bore and no-one would get seriously hurt but in High School I noticed the same fight would some-times produce broken stuff so fights were fewer but fiercer. The nastiest sight I saw was after closing time in front of the South Fork Saloon when a man repeatedly kicked his downed opponent in the head as he lay on the snowy pavement. The stories I have shared are child's play compared to some of the really vicious guys I have seen in action. There was a guy up the line named Darrel. He was not that big but there was no mercy in him. I have seen him, when confronted, break off a beer bottle and go after his opponent like "Jack the Ripper." Those kind of fight stories are no longer fun to listen to so let's explore the beautiful side of darkness;

Chapter 10 A Few Memorable Girls

This chapter is rated R skip it if that bothers you. To me the drugs, the drinking, the cars, sometimes even the fights... were all just props to chase what I was most interested in; hot girls. I do not speak frankly like this to boast but I am hoping a player like I was reads this, relates, and finds the better path I once thought was bunk.

At age 5 my Father and I were walking along the river and he picked up an old bone - probably a cow bone - and said, "Bud, back millions and millions of years ago, when mankind was first learning to walk on two legs amazing creatures like the wooly Mammoth ranged in these parts. And this is probably one of their bones! My Dad had been the valedictorian of his high school, was a successful businessman, and I was impressed. Hardly a week went by without Dad getting into his vivid descriptions of the "Big Bang Theory" or the gospel according to Darwin. With grade school textbooks and high school agnostics reinforcing my Dad's doctrine I was thoroughly persuaded that I evolved from Australapithicus and could argue my point rather persuasively. The cornerstone of evolution is survival of the fittest, so as one of the fittest, I felt it was my duty to follow my hormonal programming and perpetuate mankind. This was definitely my favorite part about the theory of evolution. My motto became "if it feels good do it!"

In the 70's Hugh Hefner's "Playboy" magazine found it's way into our home too and into my sneaky little 3rd grade mind. In about 5th grade my buddy and I took some hard core porn out behind his shed and looked it over real good. This helped pour gas on my girl crazy disposition and since my family didn't believe in the Bible or ten commandments my values were formed by Hugh Hefner.

And the only instruction on these matters my Dad ever gave me was to take a plug and tell me, "this is you" then point at the electrical receptacle and say, "this is the female" and then he plugged it in. In high school he let me know to ask him if I ever needed any condoms. My liberal moral compass where sexuality was concerned was further skewed by another class in school in which I was taught that Freud felt all human activity is motivated by sexuality and that most males think about it 90 % of the time.   This became the training I was to later live out though I was also a nice guy who treated girls well because I grew up with intelligent beautiful sisters.

As I entered Middle School some felt I had poster boy good looks and I was absolutely girl crazy... a dangerous combination that would later earn me the nickname "Bud the Stud." My first sweetheart in 7th grade was the popular blonde cheerleader I mentioned in a previous chapter. For some reason she liked the all star catcher (in baseball) in cool suede hiking boots. (These monstrous suede expedition hiking boots which were the fad in 7th grade.) I was pretty elated that I became the object of her affection. Though an older girl had talked me into kissing her at a beer party earlier that summer, Emma was the first girl I really made out with at the local theater. So heavenly to french kiss for a half hour and see the messed up blonde hair on her sweaty face. After the movie I walked down to my friends motel to spend the night and felt these strange growing lumps under my neck. Before midnight I realized I had a very bad case of the mumps. I wondered if my Grandma's prayers were laboring to spare me from this playboy path I was embarking on. But I had tasted something I really liked and was eager for more.   In retrospect I think few guys who live out the Playboy mindset come to Christ because once you have the key to the candy store it is difficult to be talked into the one and done mentality Christianity advocates.   At least that was my experience.

56

Then I entered my ivy league era when I really wasn't a corrupt guy. I had a respectable smart girlfriend for over a year and sometimes we spent hours necking and exploring each others bodies but we never actually had sex. We almost did at a house party she threw when her parents were away but as clothes were coming off someone screamed, "parents are home unexpectedly!" and I hid in the closet. She was the kind of girl a guy would want to marry but for some strange reason I wanted a girl with a more pronounced jaw line as I was attracted to that. For that silly reason I ended a great relationship with a fine friend. I guess I was still Columbus on an expedition to explore the unknown.

When I was 15 this other blonde asked me out for the Sadie Hawkin's dance. After buying me a nice dinner we went to a house party where she kept putting her hands down my pants to get what she came for. That was pretty exciting for me so I retired us to my friends basement to grant her every wish. I greatly enjoyed the night but never asked her out again. Finally her friend asked me, "Buddy did that mean anything to you or was it just a one night stand?" I answered that she was real nice but I wasn't looking at it as going steady or anything. She said "well what if she is pregnant?!" I said "well I will help provide an abortion." As a Darwinist I did not see either abortion or a tryst as out of line.

There were quite a few other babes I'd get down with but usually didn't go all the way with since we were in my pick-up or the cramped Little Green Buger. Then one night I was dancing at "The Dew Drop Inn" (a local bar) I was only sixteen but this cute 17 year old with an amazing back yard seemed really sweet on me so I asked her if she wanted to come to my house. Again I think someone was praying for me because I got my car

57

terribly stuck at the bar in a big hole but finally several tough drunks pushed me out and again I climbed over the wall of the little conscience I had left, took her home and started kissing her ash tray tasting lips. She kept tantalizing my ear with her tongue and we ended up having explosive sex. Partly why she was so good in bed was that she'd had a lot of practice. I knew a couple of the guys in our up-the-line gang had gotten down with her. But what I didn't know is that this little hottie had just come off of a road trip with a motorcycle gang! The next morning I felt inflamed in all the wrong places and it felt like creepy crawlers were biting me down there. I found out I had contacted both painful Crabs and Herpes and another STD that took 9 years to surface. The Crabs were easy enough to get rid of with Crab treatment and a shower but the Herpes were very painful and persistent. 9 years after taking this motorcycle hottie to bed another STD surfaced in me that acted like a prostate infection.   The specialist gave me a very expensive antibiotic and said there was a 50% chance I would be cured. My friend at Abbot Loop Christian Fellowship fasted and prayed for me and I was in the blessed 50% and the regimen of special antibiotics fixed me. I was embarking on a path that was becoming addictive.

I guess I was pretty dumb because many guys go years of playing around but here in my Sophomore experience I land a whole grab bag of STD's!   After getting Crabs and Herpes you would think I would be smart enough to lay off her. But she was incredible in bed so I took her out to the TeePee which my friend and I lived in on a pot farm in Swan Lake.   Big Chief had some more fun with his woman in the TeePee then as I was holding her in my arms she asked me, "Buddy do you love me?" At first I thought "of course not we're just workin' on our night moves right?" I felt like telling her "baby I don't know God and don't even know what love is but I know this isn't it." Instead I managed a weak - "I like you real well." I had many faults but I was an honest bad guy and my candid answer didn't go over real big and we never had sex again. It was an awkward moment so I grabbed my fishin' pole and went into the back yard to fish (the TeePee was on Swan River.) As I was fishing I actually felt kind of a disgust for the girl. Maybe it was really a disgust for myself... After that I wondered what real love was but I knew the lusty world of "Bud the Stud" was certainly not what love was about. I wondered what being in real love would be like. I thought to myself, "why do I feel empty after just doing what Playboy magazine touted as the pinnacle of life's joys?" Looking back on it she probably had a Dad who was never affectionate and had possibly even abused her sexually. So she was lookin' for love in all the wrong places - trying to trade sex for love and I was too honest even then to make the trade. I think we are all designed to experience God's perfect love and until we do we are trying to fill that void with the best this world has to offer; lust... but it never fully scratches the itch/ I guess it is called lust because it only leaves you wanting more. I later reflected that if she could just get to know the Heavenly Father it would be to her like a deep drink from a cool well in an arid land. (I now view love as the commitment to care for a woman and her children...emotionally and financially.... lust, on the other hand, has to do with self gratification and then just walking away.)

Another girl named --- gave me lots of joy with her amaz amazing porcelain bod. But though we got naked together and played around half the night we didn't go all

59

the way. I think after my surprise package of STD's I was reluctant to pull the trigger. She grew a little impatient with my reluctance but I never enjoyed taking a shower in a rain coat so I just played but she soon left me because to be honest I think she wanted more than that. Maybe why I just toyed with her is that I had seen a jaw dropping brunette a time or two in Whitefish that totally possessed my mind.....I became totally obsessed with a California girl that didn't seem interested in me.

To protect her identity I will call her by the nick name not many knew. Sam from L.A. was dark with naturally curly hair and a striking body that even the Playmates I drooled over in Playboy could not compare with. At first we became just friends though I had the crazy hots for her. Her Mom was leaving for a week so she wanted me to "babysit Sam" I don't know how wise it was to ask a 17 year old playboy to babysit her incredibly hot 16 year old daughter alone in her condo for 5 days! But L.A. coke dealers had a little different moral code! As Sam slept upstairs for the week I spent half the night thinking of things I would like to do with her but I wanted to be a good babysitter and frankly I don't think she wanted me in that way yet so I just took her to school each day and was a nice friend. She could have any guy she wanted and I don't think it was me that was in her sights. (This chapter may make me sound like a real slime ball but many of the girls I dated and did stuff with thought I was a real nice guy and compared to some of my friends I was. This friend of mine wanted Sam too but to him she was nothing more than a piece and to me I had a level of care for her after being her babysitter. :) She and I became friends and partied together but I don't know if she knew I was intensely crazy about her. I took her to a party in

Coram and someone put a bunch of cross tops (speed) in my beer and I really went wild and was trying to fight the biggest toughest guy at the party but rather than watching me get pulverized my friend Don took me home where I passed out. The next day I picked up Sam from the party and she had dozens of hickies all over her body. (Why didn't Sam's parent restrain her when she saw all the hickies? Because Sam was from a broken home and her Mom was a Cocaine smuggler. A sexy intelligent woman but that is how she brought home the bacon. Actually it was interesting conversing with her about exactly how she did it... she WAS intelligent! We liked to talk and once she hinted that she'd like to show me some intimate bed tricks that I could later use for her daughter. That was a little too liberal even for me so I changed the subject.

When I found out who gave Sam all the hickies I decided I better make my move on her because the hickie dude wasn't considered as good looking as me and I knew he didn't care for her at all. Then one night my good friend who wanted her was partying together with Sam and I and another girl or two and he kept trying to put his arm around her but she kept trying to just sit by me. I decided it was time to break out of friend zone so I put my arm around her and could feel some electricity in her vibe this time so I got super excited and took her home with me to my bed. I made some moves but she was a little drunk and tired and wanted to sleep. (Contrary to some beer commercials I often found alcohol counter productive to good libido.) The next morning though we awoke with that loving feeling and had a breathtaking long time together. We became lovers as well as friends but did not yet consider ourselves going together steady. I guess when you are that hot taking yourself off the market is a really big step.

It was kind of a challenge dating her because I could not even walk her in the park without other guys whistling and heckling her. (It was like the song, "When You're in Love With a Beautiful Woman….better look alive…) I took her to another party and good looking older guys were all hitting on her so hard and she was kind of liking it so I just nursed my hurt and jealously and pretended to be interested in the girls that were looking my way…. even though I wasn't. Up till then I had usually been the one breaking hearts but now I tasted the bitterness of un-requited love. I seethed inside after that party but my mind was so obsessed with her that I just kept up my cal-culated pursuit. I just kept up the nice guy friend thing but was always ready to go a little further whenever she was. That moment came when we were parked at the train depot in Whitefish thoroughly steaming up the win-dows of the little green buger. Some railroad employee kept pretending to have job duties near where we were parked so he could peer into my steamed up win-dows…….. I guess he couldn't resist trying to look at her perfect body either. By then she told me "Buddy I really like you, you are the first guy I do this with who I also feel is a true friend." So even though she didn't really take her hot commodity self completely off the market she was sort of like my girlfriend! I was the envy of every guy and I cannot deny the extreme pleasure just looking at her amazing beauty brought me.   Yet somehow I didn't feel that fulfilled deep down because we often had to be drinking or high to enjoy getting our clothes off together. I attribute that to conscience. Even though I had evolution rammed down my ears since early childhood I still had a conscience and to cross lines intended for marriage still needed something to numb the conscience before doing the deed. Dentists use Novocain we used weed, hash, cocaine, and alcohol or any mixture thereof.

Why wasn't I fulfilled? I had reached the zenith of the mountain of sexual conquest; I was sleeping with a 10! Yet somehow deep inside my chest beat a dream of having a relationship that was based on really caring for a girl. Actually even with this girl I felt some genuine care that was conflicting with the training I had received from "The Playboy Forum." The Bible says "deep calls to deep in the roar of your waterfalls." Even though I was a player who didn't really know what love was, the image of God that I'd been created in was calling out to me and when it called to me in the deepest parts of my inner man it echoed around in my empty heart and somehow showed me that there was a place of love with a woman that was like a T-bone steak compared to the cheap buffets I'd been eating. Because I just revised this chapter last night I was thinking about this subject when my wife and I just had an incredible morning fun time and when it was over I told her, "I love you so much forever baby! I will always be there for you!" And she was saying the same thing and patting me tenderly as her beautiful form still engulfed my being. As a big sex fan who has eaten

from both the table of casual sex and the table of sex within marriage I like the one where I don't need to get drunk first or shower in a rain coat so I don't pick up creepy crawlers from the girls last partner(s)! And after the act when my baby asks me if I love her I like being able to reply "yes and forever" rather than exiting the afterglow with my fishing pole !

Bud the Stud

Chapter 11..What Goes Up must come DowNNN!

(The World of Drugs)

My experience with drugs probably started with the gateway to the world of drugs which for many people is pot. (Cannabis, Ganga, Reefer, Marijuana, Weed, Bud, Nug). Since family members smoked I first tried it when I was 9 on a trip to Mexico and it didn't do anything to me. I tried it a few more times and I thought, "wow I must be immune to it because it doesn't get me high." Then there was this dorky lanky guy from South Carolina that my Dad hired one summer called Chestley. He taught us how to spit tobacco juice really far and he also got us loaded one time in the car his Grandma gave him. (It was an old four door Chevy in mint condition that was his pride and joy.) Some people need to smoke pot on several occasions before the THC really builds up in them and the desired high takes place. Well this day was the tipping point for me and wow did I get blasted! It felt so great and then and there I became a pot addict. I would carve pot leafs on my arm and put ink from my pen down into them to make tattoos on myself but they never lasted. I would draw pot leaves on my notebooks instead of paying attention in high school. I would sell joints in the bathroom between classes to spread the good news. I made beautiful deer horn pipes and sold them on commission in the local head shop. I even made the bong to end all bongs! It was called the "Big Blue Bomber." The BBB was made with a piece of blue 1 1/2 inch pvc close to three feet long. I then made a custom elk horn mouth piece out of a whopper Elk horn. My bong was pretty much regarded as the king of bongs among the peers I hung with. My Father taught me carpentry and woodworking from age 5 so I did nice work - when I was 16 he saw a collection of my antler pipes I had just put finish on. I was alarmed when he saw them but he just commented, "though I don't agree with what you are doing I must say you do nice work." My world pretty much revolved around the next high. It made me feel so good and powerful. It seemed to heighten the sensory mechanisms in my head to where sex felt better, I seemed more creative when I played blues harp, and experiences with my friends were in an elevated and electric realm.

I tried Cocaine and it really didn't do much for me.....though "cocoa puffs were nice (a joint laced with Coke) , I took acid (LSD) with my friends and got way crazier than I already was and hallucinated some but I really just did it to fit in......I thought it was crazy and really didn't like it that much. I enjoyed magic mushrooms but then had a trip that turned really scary when I was on a date with a girl named Vickie.   Speed was fun but I was a cranked up dude by nature so amping that up wasn't really what I loved. Downers blended better with my chemistry. We took big white quaaludes and sat around and said, "wow man." But what I really liked was valium. The little yellow pills would make me feel so cool and laid back and I never seemed to have a bad trip on them. I would even take them when I was alone sometimes just to chill and listen to Paul McCartney and Wings.

In some respects the scariest part of being hooked on artificial highs is when we could not afford or obtain any normal drugs. At times like that we would resort to home made solutions to get high. The one which probably destroyed more of my brain cells than any other activity was snuffing gasoline. The buzzing we experienced was in all likelihood just brain cells frying and dying! One of my best friends almost fell asleep on a 5 gallon jerry can one night and I think he might have died if I had not pried him off it ! Though Christ saved me and restored my life I still have to pray for my memory as these wasted days took their toll on my mind.

  At the end of the day though I always returned to pot, hash, and alcohol. It was really hard to beat good Sensimilla. (I think it was called that because it made the user feel like they had a million senses.....senses they never even knew they had.)   The only thing to really equal Sense was good Hawaiian. I tried other kinds, Panama Red, Columbian...just a shade above shit weed and plenty of Mexican some which had fancy names like "Mohican." By the time I got done smoking all this stuff I was like the "Last of the Mohicans:" Blasted!   When you smoke weed almost every day for years you may be flunking out of school but you should be familiar with the multifarious nature of Cannabis.   Though it is well docu- mented that many car wrecks are caused by pot the only person I ever heard of directly dying from smoking pot was a guy who smoked Cannabinoid; a man made version of Cannabis. (K-2)

  My love for pot culture got me in serious trouble with the fearsome Vice-Principal of Columbia Falls High. You got to be a bad ass dude to be a good Vice-Principal and Mr. Vincent was the epitome of a merciless hard nose who feared nothing living or dead and had quick access to a huge paddle and a variety of harsh forms of student torture and strict discipline.   I was always a smart tricky guy who rarely got caught for my misdeeds so it was no big deal for me to feign interest in

Mr. Smalley's Biology lab while pocketing choice test tubes, rubber stoppers with holes drilled in them, and flared end glass tubing which worked perfect for a pot pipe when I placed a screen in it. One of my creations was a mini bong about 10 inches tall that delivered an un-tainted glass lined hit with great precision. Back then school dances were big and we would shake our stuff or do slow dances which triggered the Tarzan and the Ma-donna in us. One night we got semi blasted with a cou-ple six packs and then tried to get in to the school dance. Mr. Vincent and some other fun stopper were at the door smelling kid's breath and stuff. When my turn came it was bad enough that he knew I'd been drinking but it really got scary when he said, "Buddy Willows I've been waitin' for you.....look what I found in your locker today, and he pulled out my prize mini-bong!!!" Someone had tipped him off and they had raided my locker! Up till that time the shadows of my previous good grades and base-ball exploits kept me from being branded a total stoner but that night every shred of good reputation vanished and I remember thinking..."Oh Shit, I am really in for it this time!"

Probably the height of my pot smoking career came when my friend and I "worked" on a Ranch up the Swan which posed as a tomato farm. They grew the most deli-cious hydroponic tomatoes. But the back greenhouse was set up to grow some of the highest quality pot I had ever used. The job had great benefits namely all the weed we could smoke and a tepee that was set up 15 feet from the Swan River..... a great place to bring that occasional hot girl. We didn't really work much but we got loaded a lot. Our bosses last name was Bader. When we took our infrequent work assignments from him we would jokingly say "Yes Master Bader we'll get right on it!!" It was a fun time but I remember not making much money and feeling kind of wasted all the time except for when I was enjoying the excellent fly fishing. I would hold my gun and boots with my teeth and swim across the Swan River to access some incredible rainbow trout fishing! I wore my gun at all times and became a damn fast gunslinger. I would amaze my buddies with my quick draw exploits! Being blessed with very fast reflexes worked well for catching baseballs or pulling a Colt revolver.

You might be thinking, "If pot helped you feel so elated and discover new senses you never knew you had why would you want to quit?" Good question. What goes up, must come down, down, down. We are created to have mental balance and by nature most of us are fairly steady emotionally. Unless we came from a war zone family or were abused as kids we have a pretty happy mindset. But when we use pot to "get high" we tweak with our mental balance and stimulate areas of our brain that make us feel happier than we ever did without it.   The problem is that this is followed by a burnt out low feeling which also makes one forgetful, sometimes paranoid, and generally lethargic. Where once you were happy without it now you need it to even feel half happy. Sure pot makes you high but it is followed by a subsequent low then you need more pot to get up again and the following lows become gradually even lower and the grade and amount of pot you need to get up again must increase for you to achieve the same high and when that is not enough you must resort to Cocaine, Crank, Crack or other heavy duty drugs to get you feeling up again.

  Though books on drugs will tell you Marijuana is not addictive it is highly addictive because once you start to use it you now need it to elevate your mood or as I stated it becomes a gateway drug because the high it produces over time may not be enough for some people. And by the time you get known as a stoner some of your good friends just aren't that interested in hanging with you anymore so you also need it because it provides a social bonfire for you and your buddies to hang around.

For these reasons I became hopelessly addicted to mostly pot. One of my favorite songs was by Jonathan Edwards, "Gonna Lay around the Shanty and get a Good Buzz On." Don't believe the crap about how it alleviates pain or has all these great benefits. The truth is when you become a stoner about all you ever have energy to build is a shanty because after you get a good buzz on all you feel like doing is laying around. (Yes there are moments of inspired creativity and a feeling like you can leap tall buildings in a single bound but the general trend for me was to dull my strong work ethic and any user if he or she is honest will admit they were far more productive without it.

I had been an all-star baseball player that some of my coaches felt could go to the next level and one coach thought I could even play pro. I was also a promising cross-country ski racer on the Columbia Falls Ski Team who had placed first in three consecutive races before I broke my leg because my stoned friend was driving too fast on black ice. Some people said the Olympics might be in my future. That was probably far fetched but I was good enough to possibly get a college scholarship. It is really fun being a top athlete. I loved traveling abroad to play baseball. Or skiing with hot girls from Norway and Sweden who had come to represent their country. But some of these great true highs were eliminated once I became a pothead. I was very smart; as a sixth grader I placed in the top 1% in the nation on the Iowa Basic Test. In 8th grade, before I became a druggee, I was a high honors student with unlimited career potential but after messing up my mind with too much hash I graduated with like a B - average, which for me was pathetic. (And I barely graduated because I skipped so much school to go party.) In the 8th grade I was respected by my whole class. By the time I graduated I was voted "The Most Spaced Out" by my class. Because what goes up must come down. People wouldn't do it if it wasn't fun and I had plenty of fun getting stoned with friends and with girls that got loose after some bud…but the messiah of marijuana and drugs left me "toasted" as a person. "Toasted" is a term we would use for when we had smoked and re smoked grass until it was nothing but ashes. That's what my once glowing life had become because of pot, alcohol, and drugs. Though I had won three races in a row and was dominating a sport I then lay fallen in a ditch with a broken femur after being ejected from a truck. I got up to rejoin my buddies and my leg collapsed under me like Jello. The first thing that came into my mind is "the cops will be coming so I better throw my weed and pipe into the field before they bust me." If I had any sense I would have thrown it into the field before my life was ruined not after. But Pot dulls your senses till you think all is fine when it is not. I call it Satan's sedative to hijack your future. But maybe you are like me and are hooked. If you can't find the brakes keep reading as the answer I found could become your answer also.

   * A comment on the legalization of Marijuana; Yes there are many Willie Nelson types who use it more responsibly and in greater moderation than I did and just

as not every person who consumes alcohol does so to their own detriment there are also those who use Pot responsibly but I am still deeply against the legalization of this dream stealer. *After one of Marijuana legalization in Colorado overall traffic fatalities in Colorado have increased by 100 percent for operators testing positive for marijuana from 39 in 2007 to 78 in 2012.*

According to the new report by the Rocky Mountain High Intensity Drug Trafficking Area entitled "The Legalization of Marijuana in Colorado: The Impact," the impact of legalized marijuana in Colorado has resulted in:

1. The majority of DUI drug arrests involve marijuana and 25 to 40 percent were marijuana alone.

2. In 2012, 10.47 percent of Colorado youth ages 12 to 17 were considered current marijuana users compared to 7.55 percent nationally. Colorado ranked fourth in the nation, and was 39 percent higher than the national average.

3. Drug-related student suspensions/expulsions increased 32 percent from school years 2008-09 through 2012-13, the vast majority were for marijuana violations.

4. In 2012, 26.81 percent of college age students were considered current marijuana users compared to 18.89 percent nationally, which ranks Colorado third in the nation and 42 percent above the national average.

5. In 2013, 48.4 percent of Denver adult arrestees tested positive for marijuana, which is a 16 percent increase from 2008.

6. From 2011 through 2013 there was a 57 percent increase in marijuana-related emergency room visits. (CSN NEWS)

Even medical Marijuana is not needed in most cases. Pumping tar and carcinogens into your body and energy sappers into your mind is not the way to get healthy. Fill your lungs with Oxygen and your mood will elevate and your body will begin healing itself. I heard presidential candidate Ben Carson state that in 2014 the U.S. national debt was greater than the Gross Domestic Product.

Having a stoned populace is not the answer for America to start producing more than we borrow.

Weed is Satan's sedative to highjack your destiny. One year after becoming a user people will say of you, "his/her get up and go got up and went!"

One of my life's biggest regrets is getting a wholesome mountain climbing childhood friend into pot with me. He became as addicted as I but never shook the habit. Later in life he had to quit pot to pass a drug test for a new vocation he was applying for. Without the mental prop of pot he flipped and shot his wife and himself. I remembered the night I and another friend pressured him into smoking with us and will regret it as long as I live. Don't tell me it is not addictive because I can count on one hand the hundreds of users I have known who ever quit like I did. (Check out my Facebook "Why Not Pot?")

We had a nice family (Jamey, Sharlon, and I above) but once parental separation and paralysis of my mother struck - a chaotic lack of supervision ensued and became a breeding ground for my escalating drug use.

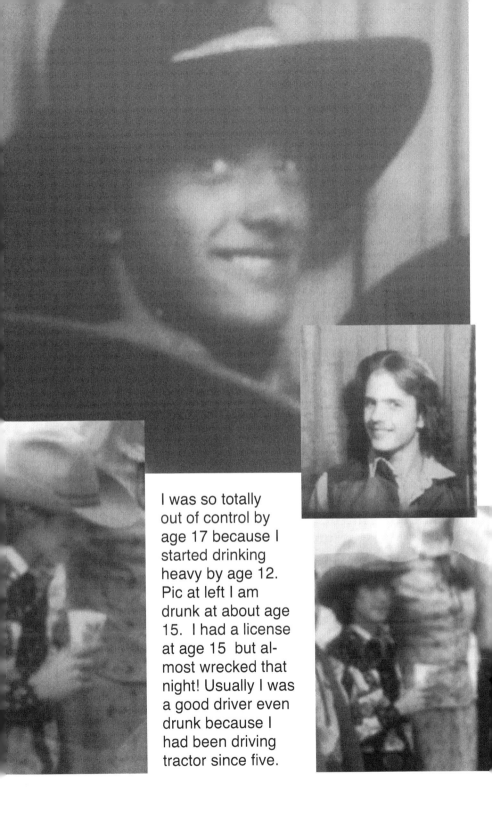

I was so totally out of control by age 17 because I started drinking heavy by age 12. Pic at left I am drunk at about age 15. I had a license at age 15 but almost wrecked that night! Usually I was a good driver even drunk because I had been driving tractor since five.

12. Totally Out of Control

I woke up on the cold grass..... I was shivering.   I shook my hungover head as I tried to recognize where in the world, or out of the world I was. Had I died and been re-incarnated on Jupiter? I felt half dead and there was a haze of gritty moon dust in the air. I finally recognized the swing set and our back porch.   I was in my back yard!! Vague memories of the wild keggar I held in the garage of my house bubbled up from my torched brain. When I opened the door to my garage the acrid stench of after keggar sickened my stomach but there were my good buddies faithfully passed out in various places in the room that was lined with my centerfold pin ups. Oh no! some fool had stolen my Stihl O-31 chain saw! ?#%*   My life seemed as hazy as the day. It was the morning after Mount Saint Helens had blown its top covering the north-west with volcanic dust.

That was just one time out of many that I felt out of control. Two other times made me feel like I was almost possessed by the Devil. One time was on Halloween night when I was about 12. A gang of us boys raised all kinds of hell. We shot out streetlights, we rolled people's spare tires down a big hill and then we got a bunch of soap and headed over to the Hungry Horse Grade School. The five of us proceeded to write cuss words on every single win-dow in the whole school. When we were done defacing the 100 or so windows we walked triumphantly off into the night. A cop approached us 8 minutes later asking about the incident but he could not prove anything so he let us go. I liked Van Halen's song "Runnin' With the Devil" but I didn't even believe in God or the Devil even though on his special day I often acted just like him! Another incident I felt out of control was when a Christian missionary visited my home and was inside Jamey's room trying to sign her and I up for some Bible course. An uncontrollable laughter came over me and then Jamey too and we just laughed uncontrollably in the guys face for at least 10 minutes till he left. It was like a demon was living on the inside. (you can almost see that in me in pic on page 69) On another occasion Jimmy Grant took me to the Catholic Church and I started laughing uncontrollably and had to leave the service. The young lads dressed in white linen like fairies was just more than I could stomach and it triggered the outburst but looking back on it I have to wonder if some evolution loving church hating evil force had taken up residence inside of me.

Much of this craziness was fun... fast cars, fast girls, buffed arms, feeling a part of the "up-the-line" gang. There was camaraderie similar to what I imagine a motorcycle gang might experience. We all had our names and nick-names and fighting reputations and it was fun being one of the "Canyon Sultans." Something I was known for is that I could usually win the guzzling competitions. We would grab a big beer or a fifth of tequilla and see who could down it the fastest. I could open up my throat and pour so I usually won. I was getting quite a reputation.... for all of the wrong things! Once when I was daydreaming in class I calculated that if you stacked up all the cans of beer I had drank end to end and on top of each other you could build a large three bedroom house out of beer cans !

All this was fun at first but as the wasted days turned into wasted months and drunken years somewhere along the line it dawned on me that I was no longer using the booze and the drugs but the booze and the drugs were using me. At first they came along saying, "have a few beers it will make you feel good." They were right it did make me feel good and it was fun but after awhile it took a twelve pack or some crazy combination of alcohol, pot and maybe some acid to experience the same feeling of wild elation the previous weekend had held. But most of those Friday or Saturday nights ended up with my face in the porcelain throne as I puked my guts out before going to a bed that was spinning so bad I would have to put my hand on the ground to slow it down. Drugs and alcohol were now the master and I was the slave. I became painfully aware of the strength in the grip of my new slave-master one night when we were all partying up in Coram and suddenly I became a complete animal. I vaguely remember picking a fight with this monstrous buffed guy…I remember it didn't go real well for me but then all went blank. After a drunk details of the night before emerge slowly but this time details were almost non-existent. Later I was told that the reason I went so wild is that a Coram kid had spiked my beer with too many crosstops (speed). My buddy had been nice enough to take me home out of harms way but later that night he smashed up one side of my truck because I think he may have had a few too many too. I took pride in my Blue 1971 Dodge truck with Holley carb and dual exhaust so I felt pretty bad the next morning when both I and my truck were smashed.

The "wasted days and wasted nights" culture has plenty of good-hearted, well meaning people in it (and that is why many stay in it for social needs that church can just as easily supply.) While many are 'good people" there are also some sicko's!; At one keggar in Coram I remember seeing a two year old still in pampers that the parents were giving beer to drink. Then I overheard the guy brag to someone; "sometimes I put my cigarette out on his arm." I saw the round burn marks on the kids arm from where he had done this and I got angry.

It became a little scary to me when many mornings I had to be told what I actually did the night before because I had been so out of it. If you have ever been in the throes of addiction you just shake yourself now and then to make sure you are still in touch and haven't done anything to land you in prison. One morning like that I woke up with a terrible hangover and looked out my window and my truck was gone! I began freaking out and I think I called the police because I was sure someone had stolen it! I tried real hard to remember who I was with the night before and then called up Jay on the phone? "Do you remember what we did with my truck Jay?" After his fog cleared he said, "I think we just walked home Bud!" Sure enough we made our way back up to the South Fork Saloon, in Martin City, and there was my stolen truck!!! Right where we had left it the night before because we were too drunk to remember we had a truck! :) It was probably a good thing we forgot we had it or we may have wrecked.

I have always been an entrepreneur but in this era my skills were being used to create deer horn pipes that I sold on commission in the local music store. On the side I would sell what went in them. I was mostly a small time dealer who just sold enough to supposedly support my own habit but my friend was a bigger wheel. Just a couple weeks before I came to Christ we were partying in his red Dodge Dart while we had a half pound of high grade Hawaiian bud in a backpack. The cop came up and wanted to know what we were doing. Our buddy adroitly had gotten out of the car with a gallon milk jug and said, "officer could you possibly help me get some gas ?, I just ran out! We breathed a sigh of relief because the officer fell for it which gave us 3 others a chance to chuck our open beers, paraphernalia and hide the half pound of pot!

77

When I think of the mercy of God I think of him not allowing me to get caught that day because I was already a centimeter away from being sent to boy's prison for at least 6 months and with intent to distribute on my robust record I could have been incarcerated for a good while.

This life of not being able to find the brakes had been going on and getting more intense since the summer of my 12th year and now I was 17. I felt like the guest in the Eagles Hotel California" song because I came into the world of drug and alcohol abuse anytime I wanted but now I could never leave no matter which new mantra I chanted or which yoga position I engaged in. The ugly climax to this "stairway to heaven" was when I was staying with my good mates Donny and Roger Hale in a little apartment across from the "Deer Lick Bar" in Martin City. Friday and Saturday had been non stop binge drinking and I woke up on the keggar soaked carpets with a pounding headache and a dry acrid hang-over. I didn't feel right and went to the filthy john and puked a little more. But this time my stomach was already emptied and dry heaves continued till only blood was coming out of my mouth. When the ordeal subsided I got up off the cheap linoleum, which smelled of piss, and looked at myself in the mirror and pointed my finger at my tired ashen face and said, "Buddy Willows you had better find a way out of this lifestyle or you are going to be dead!"

apt. where I was at the time at left

It was on Main ST. near our favorite Bar (above)

Chapter 13   Searching

That was the beginning of sensing a need for change. I was seventeen and it was summer and my resolve didn't really lead to any changes other than I started reading about Metaphysics. I would sit out in the trees and read these college level dissertations on scientific Metaphysics. it took a while to get through the elevated language but I eventually discovered mind power and visualizing the healing or the result you desire was at the core of this philosophy. For me it didn't hold much power or answer fundamental questions so my search continued.

I then read a spiritual book called "Siddhartha" by Herman Hesse. Siddhartha's journey basically culminated in learning to meditate and empty his mind of all thought as he chanted a peaceful OMMM! I began meditating and discovered that in that meditative state I could begin to control bodily functions that I had heretofore never been able to control. In a yoga position meditating I could speed my pulse up till it was rapid or slow it down as if my heart and pulse were on a magical dial which my meditative consciousness controlled. My girlfriend Sam and her brother Todd thought this was super cool! There was some power in it as one cool dude I knew actually changed the color of a precious stone in his ring just by meditative concentration of psychic power. I thought Siddhartha's journey was interesting and found meditation cool but it didn't answer my real questions like, "who am I?, where did I come from?, where am I going?, is there an afterlife?" I looked at my dog Blue who would move his eyelids and mouth as he dreamed and wondered if there was a difference between men and dogs in terms of what happened after death… questions abounded answers were few.   I became strangely drawn to Bob Dylan's new album "Slow Train Coming."

One song said, "you gotta serve somebody....it might be the Devil, or it may be the Lord but you gotta serve somebody."   Another song said, "you got to do unto others like you'd have them, oh like you'd have them.... do unto you."   I thought that was a great saying and had no idea that it came from the Bible, because I had never read the Bible, but I intentionally tried to start living that way. I would consciously try the "do unto others" routine but I found there was an inner selfishness in me which so often kept me falling short of that ideal.   I would try to let my friend have the first toke of prime bud but I often just lit it up myself.   One of my friends said girls were just life support systems for pussies. When I sifted that anecdote with the grid of my new "do unto others" thought it seemed like such a sick and twisted thought even though I was still girl crazy and I still drank and smoked pot way too much.

My sister kept telling me the answer lay in "Black Elk Speaks" which chronicle stories of a Sioux sage which saw visions of the future.   The mystical visions of the future held a wow factor but I was basically just as addicted as I was before reading it and even though he could see the future my future looked pretty blurry and I was curious about what happened after death.

To me the Bible was just a collection of wishful thinking and fairy tales so I never recalled reading it except when Dan and I used a verse in Genesis about God giving man "herb bearing seed" to win our 7th grade debate that Marijuana should be legalized. Christian religion didn't impress me much either. One time after Joe and I got in the fight I described earlier, where the dude gave Joe a concussion with the torque wrench, Joe and I were going out to party and avenge our losses the next weekend. On our way to the fighting grounds Joe said, "Bud I gotta stop by church and confess before we go out." I waited in his hot Ford truck while he went in. When he came out I asked, "Joe what did you do in there anyway?" He said "I went in there and met with the father, who sits in a booth behind a curtain. I confessed my sins to the father and he forgave me." "You didn't tell him what we have been doing and what happened last weekend did you?!!!" "Well not specifically but I gave him the abbreviated version." "And then you are just going to go out and party and fight some more with me tonight?" "Well ya we don't really have to change as long as we confess and get forgiveness." I replied, "I don't know anything about religion but that just doesn't seem to me like the way religion is supposed to work." Another time I went with my girlfriend to a Lutheran lock in where all us middle schoolers were locked in a church all night. To me it was childish and boring and was like a party with no beer and no place to make out. I was not at all impressed with religion.

Then came a title I laughed about outwardly but inwardly scorned. It came at the time when we seniors in Columbia Falls High school voted for the most popular, the best looking, the funniest kid in the senior class for the annual. Well my peers voted me as "the most spaced out." I thought I was just a somewhat tough crazy girls guy stoner but knowing my peers now perceived me as "the most spaced out" kid in class was kind of a rude awakening. I found myself missing the "Buddy Willows" who was a high honor role student in 8th grade and before that was always in the top 3% in the nation on test scores. I found myself missing the all-star catcher in baseball and the cross-country ski racing champion. The song said, "I wanna rock n roll all night, and party every day." But after doing it for 6 years every weekend and almost every day in the summer I was beginning to look for a way out but I was trapped. I was addicted to alcohol, drugs, immoral sex, and the whole party scene. For me it seemed there was no way out just a few sane days before the next out of control binge. Black Elk could foretell the coming of the white man but no one had an answer to my addictions. Meditation might offer inner sanctum and abilities to control my pulse but no power to change my life where the rubber met the road.

So far my search had just added a dreamy philosophical aura to the still wild and crazy Buddy Willows.

Grizz got poisoned by this time because he was kind of a hell raiser too. And I really missed him ! My Dad had Grizz and I painted in a mural that now graces the West wall of my business Willows HuckLand. (Above)

Chapter 14 The Strong Arm of the Law

If you and i just evolved from Apes why should we ob-
serve any set of moral regulations? So we can be a good
ape?   if we came about when the sun hit the primordial
soup and our existence would be over with our last
breath then why regulate moral behavior? The logical
deduction I made from my evolution based world view
was"if it feels good do it." So that became my guiding
principle.   Not one time had I ever heard of anything
such as the ten commandments.

So I began to steal. I watched my friend get caught
shoplifting so I determined I would get good at it and I
did. The first thing I stole was when I was 7 and wanted
to get my Dad a nice fathers day present. I took a big
mallard duck pen holder off the dime store shelf and
pulled the unit inside my coat. I was trembling when I
walked out but I remember Dad was touched by my gift.
Next came my need for fishing lures and candy bars. I
was smart and careful and stole several thousand dollars
of stuff from stores over the next ten years. The only
scare came when a friend named Bob and I stole some
larger ticket items from the sporting goods section of a
store during our lunch break in the 8th grade.   (Even the
Ivy League 8th grader still had some wild friends from up
the line.) I made a clean getaway but as Bob came out
loaded right behind me, a store manager came running
out after him and grabbed ahold of him. Bob wheeled
around and kicked the man hard right in the nuts! Then
we split. I never did get caught for shoplifting but I often
noticed that when I stole I would often lose other things I
owned which were more valuable than the the things I
stole! I called it karma. The thieving escalated one night
when Bob and I broke into a house and stole valuables

but I felt the stakes were too high and never did that again. Shoplifting was my gig.   Then my good hunting buddy told me his strategy for us to become rich. He figured out that on Thursdays all the money from the circle K convenience stores is taken to the main store for pickup. He told me "Bud I will walk in with a mask and gun and hold them up and I just need you to be nearby in my truck then when I come running out you come wheelin' in for our getaway and we will both have all the money we need for drugs and everything else!" I looked at him and said,   "we have been through lots together and got away with a good bit but this time you are going too far for even me!!"   I didn't drive but he went ahead with the job. But when he did the clerk would not give the tall skinny dude in the mask the money!   My friend waved the gun around long enough for her to finally give him the money but by then the cops were waiting in the parking lot!   He went to boys prison for 6 months and the guy who drove for him got caught too. I was glad I sat that gig out!

Though I never got caught for shoplifting I was caught at school for making the pot pipe from Mr. Smalley's biology lab. Then I got caught at least twice for underage drinking which sometimes led to being detained at the police station.   And I got caught and spent a night in jail for vandalizing the signs in the aforementioned story. By the time I was 17 I had so many large and small run ins with the authorities that the police and my parole officer told me, "Buddy you are a habitual offender on parole. If we catch you doing ANYTHING else…even Jaywalking across the street you are going to Pine Hills (boys prison) for six months!" Even that very legit threat could not curb my behavior…I had the desire at times to change but not the power to change. Oh well, most of my friends had been to boys prison already so it wasn't the end of the world. I partied on but began to wonder if a person like me could EVER change!

My Dad took me to the A & W and had a talk with me about how bad my reputation was becoming and urged me to change. I never forgot that and appreciated the time he took to do so. If he lived with us and provided some guidelines it probably would have helped. Divorce and separation is a great way to get the one guy who can help most, Dad, out of the picture. It is not my inten-

tion to dishonor him in this book. He was a really fun, smart, man who taught me to be a good carpenter and a hard worker. And though he desperately needed anger management classes he had a fun side that I definitely inherited by osmosis ! Dad's radiance helped him start and run for 30 years the business which is now called "The Huckleberry Patch."

Chapter 15   A Night to Remember

In January of 1981 Roger Walters and other school
mates told me a dream that Pastor George Moore from
the "Hungry Horse Chapel" told them he had recently
experienced. They told me he dreamed that I was
brought into the church on a stretcher and the congregation gathered around me in prayer and encouragement
and then I rose up off the stretcher and started to praise
God. When my buddies told me the dream I snorted,
"who does that fat preacher think he is? Telling his stupid dreams around town!" But within a week something
happened which made me think I could have really been
being brought into his church on a stretcher;

Scotty and I were out in the "Little Green Buger" partying
In Columbia Falls on a Friday night. Just raising hell and
listening to my crystal clear 200 amp car audio belt out
"Cocaine" by Eric Clapton. But then the "Little Green
Buger" died and would not start again. As I pulled over
Scotty asked, "what do we do now Bud?" "Aw let's go on
in to Whitefish and see if we can find my girl Sam and
see what's goin on." "OK!" came Scott's typical good na-
tured Irish response.   We stuck our thumbs out across
from "Todd's Night Owl" and a blue Ford pickup stopped
to pick us up. I turned to Scott, "I don't think I wanna get
in ....that's Tom Brake the Jesus freak." But then we
looked in and there was Mark Schaefer who was one of
our Canyon gang so we thought it would be OK. Mark
was a blondie from a big family in Coram and we liked to
play foosball and race each other home from "The Palm"
Disco in Whitefish.   Scott and I jumped in and sure
enough Tom started in with the Jesus crap. As I was
about to spit out some of my well rehearsed evolution
lines Mark piped up

86

and said, "Bud, you should listen to this because I just found out it is all REAL!" He continued, "last weekend I was at a big party in Whitefish and someone spiked my drink with an overdose of "Purple Dragon" acid. When it took effect I found myself dying. I could smell an odor like burning flesh.....it was like when you put your lighter under human hair. And then the room grew a dingy red color. I knew I was dying and going to Hell." I listened. "Then this dude came up to me and said, 'Mark if I was you I would call out to Jesus - just call out to Jesus for help.' I don't even know why he told me to do that because he was not a church person at all. So I called out to Jesus and when I did the throbbing effects of the acid immediately left my mind, the smell and color of the gates of hell left, and a bright blue light came into the room displacing the dingy red glow. I felt strong and pure and I walked out of that bedroom into the main room of the party, where some immoral stuff was taking place, and people recoiled away from the holy presence that was upon me." I replied, "maybe you were just tripping out on acid Mark!" He replied, "I have taken plenty of acid on many other occasions but this time the effect of the acid was totally erased when I came to know Jesus!" Mark was always a pretty bubbly boy but now he was really beaming! He had that same radiant power look that Tom was glowing with!

I thought, "WOW that sounds like a real spiritual power doing a real thing in someone I know to be a cool dude!" Inside I was thinking.....I am searching for a real power that could set me free from this addicted, destructive life I am living...I am searching for truth. Scott said something about how God had changed his cousin Jimmy in a similar way. I winced when I thought my party hardy pard might be leaning the Jesus way and then Tom picked up the conversation. "Buddy, God has a plan for your life and when you give your life to Jesus you find the plan for your life and it fits just right like a hand fitting into a glove!" I usually blew Tom off but there was a glow all over his face and eyes as he spoke and I could feel a clean wave of power coming off him. For once I listened without my usual smart-alek remarks. As we arrived in Whitefish they told us, "why don't you come to this Christian coffee house just off Main Street. There is music and donuts and a lot of people that have been born again." To me it sounded lame so I said "thanks you guys maybe another time."

We walked to her house to find Sam but she was out partying. But we found her brother Todd and some other friends and soon we were getting loaded and cruising Main. The throaty roar of dual exhaust, the pulsating truck speakers blaring "The Rolling Stones," and "Van Halen." The cat-calls and course shouts. The sounds of our Friday night party ritual echoed off the 2 story bars and saloons which lined the Main Street of Whitefish, Montana. We liked to cruise Main then turn around up by the train depot. After we turned around we parked Todd's Volkswagon Rabbit and two burly guys came up to our passenger window and started angrily getting in our face. Our friend Charlie Herron was in the passenger seat closest to the guys when suddenly the biggest guy reached right in the window, grabbed Charlie by his coat and pulled him out of the window! As soon as they had him out in the open they punched and kicked him into the sidewalk then left. It all happened quick and then it was over. They f---ed him up pretty bad so we took him to Todd's place, bandaged him up, then walked back out to Main to see what other excitement we could find in the post mid-night party town.

We saw Mark Schaeffer and Alan Birky from the Coffee shop so we stopped at the corner to shoot the breeze with them. There was an evil feeling in the air that night. If music would have been playing it would have been the kind of music they play right before the shoot out at the OK Corral. A glossy black Chevy step-side pickup with monster tires pulled up and the driver demanded that I and my five mates tell him where Todd was. Todd was my friend that dealt Coke and these crazed dudes were obviously out to revenge a deal gone bad. They had blood in their eye so neither Scott nor I told them of Todd's whereabouts. They didn't like when I evaded their question and the driver got out aggressively with fire in his eyes and yelled "you punks better get the H--- out of here and quick." Danny said he or his friend was waving a gun around at this point. I was pretty tough or pretty dumb and didn't run from hardly anybody, especially when Scott was at my side, so I strode calmly out into the middle of Main Street and squared my shoulders like Wyatt Earp to meet them. As their leader walked up to meet me our eyes locked in combative disdain. I noticed he was older and bigger than me but that had never stopped me before. He grabbed me by the collar and pulled back his fist to nail me. I glanced behind him to see his massive hulking side-kicks waiting to assist him; one of them had a big bore pistol aimed at my head. When I turned to face him I imagined that Scott would be on my right and my other 4 friends would be behind me ready to rumble. To my alarm I glanced around and my friends were no-where to be seen! .....the gun must have scared them off. I quickly decided, "this is no time to fight, this is a time to talk...and fast." I said, "Why don't you just let me go, I'm not the one you are looking for." He let me go and being a little too stoned I stupidly leaned over to pick up my fallen

Stetson party hat. As I was coming up with it I saw his fist flying toward my face so I leaned back hard to evade the blow. This left my midsection unguarded and his steel toed logging boot came up with full force right into my groin..... The blow sent a paralyzing wave of blazing pain through my core and I crumpled onto the pavement while trying to protect my head from additional blows. I rolled over, sprang up and ran off into the night, "why did all my friends ditch me when I needed them the most......it could have been a good fight with six of us and four of them" I thought as I ran. My amigos talked so tough but when 4 older, bigger guys with a gun came up I guess my buddies figured that was more than they wanted a part of and I can understand that.

Cocky Buddy Willows was finally humbled. I ran down main street and into the ditch that paralleled Hwy. 93. I ran through the ditch for a long ways and finally found Scott who was also in the ditch. Scott was Hell-on-wheels when it came to fighting but even he was scared that night and whenever a set of real high headlights came our way we split. We walked and hitch-hiked out of town but nobody would pick us up even when we got clear out to the junction of Hwy. 40. To our great relief someone stopped and it was Scott's cousin Jimmy.   The whole Downing clan was famous for being tough but Jim and his brother Mike had really made the headlines by besting two car loads of cops who had billy clubs. But tough guy Jim was now all excited about Jesus too! He looked me dead in the face and said, "Buddy I saw you out there in that fight and one of those guys had a 357 magnum pointed right at your head, where would you be right now if he would have pulled the trigger?" After suppressing the urge to say, "why didn't you help me if you saw me?" I told him, "If what you Christians say is true I would be in Hell right now." He answered "That's right but it doesn't have to be that way, Jesus bled and died for you on the cross to take your sins away forever so that you could be clean and forgiven in God's sight!" When this happens it is called being "born-again" and when you get it God's power comes upon you to help you get free from drugs and alcohol and live a new life." I always thought Jim was a pretty cool guy so I really listened. I found I was more receptive after getting the hell kicked out of me earlier that night. He dropped me off and my buddies who had split came over to see if I was still alive. Mark's fervor for Christ had rubbed off on some of the others and some of them remarked that God was knocking real loud on my door so I better answer it......I wasn't too sure about suddenly believing in something I had always scorned but I was no longer a proud mocker. The next morning I woke up and thought to myself, "I could have been killed last night. I could've been wounded and on that stretcher that the Pastor saw in his dream...... I better take this God stuff more seriously because I feel like God is zoning in on me." When I was 12 years old my two best sources for presents,; Mom and Grandma, both gave me a Bible for Christmas. I was so sullen and disheartened...it was by far my worst Christmas ever. I put them neatly on the bottom of my bookshelf and just kept reading my Playboys instead. I thought that if a bad guy like me ever opened a Bible I might get struck by lightning so I carefully avoided the holy books. But that morning I had an urge to find my Bibles. I opened one of them for the very first time and I opened right up to, "The fear of the Lord is the beginning of wisdom." I had always thought Jesus was an effeminate looking guy in a sheet or maybe a felt cut out with a lamb on his head. Now suddenly I realized God was a mighty and real power that I better not scoff at or mess with anymore! I carried myself with a respect for God from that moment on. I was amazed when I got a buddy to drive me to the "Little Green Buger" later that day. We had a tow chain and I expected to tow it home. Instead it started and ran just fine! That made me feel like God was the director who purposely set the whole stage up the night before just to get my attention.

MANY MEN WANTED TO BE GOD

ONLY ONE GOD BECAME MAN

92

I'd been in plenty of scrapes but for the next two weeks I seemed to be fighting against God like that guy Jonah who got swallowed by a whale in the Bible. I still thought evolution was probably true, I still wasn't quite sure if the mountains and the creation and stars were God or if Jesus was a separate entity from them. But one thing I knew that I knew is that God Almighty had orchestrated the night to remember in such a way as to bring me face to face with a strong Christian witness and to kind of give me an ultimatum that I was called to serve him and that the road I was on was a reckless path that could lead me to an early grave at the hands of thugs, drugs, or another car wreck....I had already been in four car wrecks that were bad enough to kill a man plus some fender benders. I was also now aware that the end result of my reckless path was probably hell.

Tom, Mark, and Jim Downing realized God was dialing my number so every few days they urged me to become a Christian but I just kept telling them, "I think what you say is probably true but I am just not ready yet." I was almost sick of partying though so I told my best mates Scotty and Dan, "I am going to party hardy one more weekend with you guys and then I think I am going to probably become a Christian." We had tickets to the "Molly Hatchet" concert in Missoula so we stocked up on weed, hash, whiskey, cocaine and anything else we could think of and headed out in Dan's red Dodge Duster. On the way we drove down by "Melita Island" on Flathead Lake and got the party started with some hashish and whiskey.   I tried to hoot and cuss like normal but it felt like I might be in for another divine set up.

When we were done toking up Dan's car wouldn't start. We decided to split up into pairs and thumb a ride to Missoula. Dan and Mike Johnson would hitch hike together and Scotty and I would put our thumbs out too. A cold north wind with snow that was blowing horizontally ripped into us as we tried to hitch hike to Missoula. I had a ripped up single layer Levi jacket on and the Arctic air blast slammed through the rips in my jacket like Frank Gore facing a weak defensive front. I had dressed to party in a hotel not to brave an arctic blast! I had never read the story of Jonah and the whale but I felt like telling my mates, "if you would just ditch me you could have a great party but since God is hounding my every step you won't have fun as long as I am with you." After I felt sure that I would freeze some bleary eyed beer drinker finally picked us up and was nice enough to drop us off at the "Adam's Field House" in Missoula. We excitedly walked in to hear my favorite band and the lead singer was just strumming the last chord on the last song! Our "Up the Line gang" had all booked motel rooms together so we made our way to the cheap motel and all sat around in a circle getting loaded. Before I would have been guzzling tequila with a wild whoop, and hustlin' chicks and being a ringleader in the mayhem. But this night some unseen force in my heart caused me to see the whole scene so differently. I looked at one of the older leaders of our gang and thought, "that guy has good enough looks to take Hollywood by storm and yet here he sits just leading us all to drink enough beer to poison us for a lifetime." I looked to his left and saw another guy I had always looked up to because he drove a cool Trans Am and gave us acid. I thought to myself, "this guy could be a successful businessman but instead he is wasting his giifts on selling drugs and is surrendering his brain cells to acid

94

and alcohol. Hitching a ride back to Hungry Horse was just as bad as getting to Missoula. We got a ride with some guy from the Flathead Indian Reservation. He was wearing only tattoos and a tank top! He was pretty messed up and I was getting even more disgusted with the whole lifestyle I once thought was so cool. By the time I got home I was sick and had a fever. I was laying in the bed busted, disgusted, sick, and with an ear ache and who would drive up but Mark Schaeffer in his van. He had just come from a Jesus retreat with Tom and he was like a guy on speed he was so excited about the Lord. His convincing joy and buoyancy contrasted annoyingly with my hung over sickness but it was somehow nice to see him. He said, "Bud you told us you would come to Christ after one more big party...here is how you do it." He told me "If you confess with your mouth , Jesus is Lord," and believe in your heart that God raised him from the dead, you will be saved." (Romans 10:9 NIV) He urged me to repeat a prayer after him. At first I used the "I'm just not quite ready yet line." But he told me, "You said you would be ready after one more party and you don't look so good, I think its time!" I nodded and asked him to lead me in the prayer; "Father in Heaven, I come to you as a sinner, But I thank you that you sent Jesus your Son to die on the cross to take my sins away. I believe you did that for me Jesus. And then you rose up from the grave on the third day, so that I can rise up from the death of addiction and sin and have power to live a new life. Thank you Father that I have now become your son and I now confess that Jesus is my Lord!" I was used to taking drugs that gave you an immediate stimulus so I thought the prayer didn't work for me when no buzz, or supernatural twang hit me. After I said it I thought I would at least see a vision or get goose bumps but nothing really happened in my emotions. I just didn't feel so

so sick anymore and thanked Mark for coming and then I
went to sleep. The next day I just didn't feel like getting
stoned - which was a thrice a day ritual. That night I just
didn't feel like looking at my Playboy's - which was also a
daily ritual. I had a more peaceful sleep than usual.
Though at the time I was disappointed that the prayer was not accompanied by a drug like experience in retrospect I realize that the real miracle is that the wild and
crazy Buddy Willows was radically different within even a
few days. I thought to myself, why did this prayer change
me so much but it doesn't seem to work at all on other
people who say It? Why ? I think the answer lay in the
fact that for me "the prayer" was a surrendering moment.
Though the prayer was uneventful in the sensory realm it
was my surrender flag from a life of pride, partying and
womanizing and when I waved the white flag I really was
asking Jesus Christ to sit on the throne of my heart. In
this inner civil war my pride and desire to party had been
beaten after realizing how enslaved to pot and the bottle I
really was. The "night to remember" was my Gettysburg
where the will to fight God had been dealt a great injury.
The Molly Hatchet concert night was my last foray similar
to the guerrilla warfare of William Quantrill but now even
Quantrill's army lay banished and their leader dead. So
when I finally prayed the prayer I had thoroughly ex-
hausted every option of resistance to the King's government and was ready to lay down my grey uniform and put
on the union blue if I had to. I felt a bit like Paul must
have felt when he got knocked off his donkey and became blind. I had surrendered and unseen angels were
attending to what was left of my mind and body. I nour-
ished my emaciated spirit with the milk of God's word.

Chapter 17 Waking Up Different

Usually before school I would load up my bong, "The Big Blue Bomber" and have a hit before school. Or else meet with my mates and toke up a little. Always by lunch hour I had some T.H.C. in my veins. But for some reason I just didn't feel like smoking Nug that day. Before "the prayer" I would try everything I could think of to avoid bud for a day or two; I was a cross-country ski racer so I would tell myself how bad it was for my lungs and try so hard to avoid it but to no avail! I had been chained, I was a prisoner to addictions I seemed to have no control over. People knew me as one of the worst teen-age alcoholics in that part of the country. I'd sniff gas, snort coke, drop acid, guzzle Tequila, chew Copenhagen, toke joints or even snuff "Pam" spray to get high but now I was going a whole day and didn't even seem to need it or want it. If I was with my friends and they passed a joint my way I'd still puff some but for the most part I just didn't need to scratch that itch anymore. What happened to me anyway? I went to bed after saying a prayer with no tingles or nothing and woke up like a new person! From that day to this I have never craved either drugs or alcohol! I was chained and Jesus set me free!

For about three days I often even felt a strong spiritual force similar to a drug high but much cleaner. After a drug high I usually felt drained and in need of more drugs but after this dose of whatever it was I felt lifted inside, clean, and empowered. But after a few days, when the feeling started to subside, I began to have doubts that anything at all had really happened.In that frame of mind I developed an acute and throbbing earache. I often had horrendous ear aches growing up. In distressing pain I opened my Bible and read a verse then asked Jesus to heal me and the ear ache went away and never came back!

I told many of my old friends that since I didn't like Pot any more I was going to give away all my bongs and pipes one night after school. Some were baffled at my change but they all came over for the free auction! It was like the reading of a will to a bunch of greedy kids because I had some high quality paraphernalia! I also gave away my Penthouse and Playboy magazines. All this happened in about a weeks time and the news of my change had infected our high school. The principal John Giacomino called my pastor George Moore up and said, "Pastor WHAT DID YOU DO to that Buddy Willows?!! Could you come do it to some more of these kids!" Pastor replied, "I didn't do anything, Jesus changed his life!" Several people at church thought I was faking it and predicted I would be back on the streets in three weeks but I proved them wrong because Mike Moore told me, " Buddy you can do this just make sure to be in Church every Sunday and to read your Bible every day." I have followed that practice without missing more than one service in 35 years and God has used this routine to keep me on track. The Bible says "He who began a good work in you will be faithful to complete it." (Philippians 1:6 KJV)

I had never heard of Jesus getting hold of people that were considered hip and cool before but now there was me, Mark, Jim Downing, Danny Seliger, and Dana Overcast all miraculously changed! This made me pretty sure Jesus was coming again before the end of the year so I looked for every opportunity to shout it from the rooftops.

Often when I got the guts to finally open my mouth to talk to someone about it this supercharged tangible presence of God came over me. (Now I know it was the Holy Spirit.) As I would gush hardened people would really begin to listen or in some cases tell me to F off. Some loved me and others avoided me; one close friend I had been pretty tight with since age 5 but now he avoided me like the plague and we didn't see each other for about 5 weeks! Finally I found out where he was living and went over to say hi but I could tell he didn't want to see me or hear me talk about the big change. Other old mates listened intently to me and came with me to Christian movies and outreaches. Since I kinda lost some close mates it was nice to have Mark Schaeffer to serve God with. We both went from crazy party animals to crazy Jesus boyz. We were higher than a kite on God's new wine and we just went around laughing and telling people how much Jesus could change their life if they would just turn from their low life and say that prayer we had both prayed. Some said they weren't ready but many people did.

Since God intercepted me outside of church walls at first I wasn't too sure I needed church. But Mark and Dana persuaded me to go.   The Hungry Horse Chapel was pretty cool because there were a number of wild child Jesus converts and we were on fire with an urgent message that we were sure was going to turn the world around. The third week I was there Pastor George called on me and I said a few words about how God was changing me. He told me later that when I first walked in the doors the Holy Spirit told him, "there he is just like in the dream, not on a physical stretcher but he is a spiritual stretcher case!" I was but the prayer and encouragement I received at the church helped me rebuild my self esteem and find friendship on those lonely friday and saturday nights. Tom Brake lived above the church and one night after I stayed over with him he even confronted me about why I didn't use deodorant or wear underwear and my conversion even changed in that department!

On February 17, about two weeks after God changed my life, I hiked down to the South Fork river and sat down on a rock in the winter sun and started singing a praise song to the Lord. Then a beautiful Monarch Butterfly fluttered into view and landed on my finger! I watched its detailed pastel hairs shifting in the gentle wind. I thought it was cool and just kept praising the Lord! Later I told some friends at church how cool it was and they said, "Buddy there are no butterflies out in Montana in February, It must have been a sign from God about you being born again because the butterfly is also a born again creature. (Born first as a caterpillar, born again as a butterfly.) I realized they were right and thought it was pretty cool. We are all born once like a caterpillar crawling on the ground only seeing the things which are on the ground. But when the Spirit gives birth to us then we can enjoy a whole new dimension of life. Flight! Asking Jesus to come into your heart in a personal and intimate way allows us to be born again. If this prayer is accompanied by surrender to His Lordship, like I described earlier, new life will not only begin but continue. I realized that day that the reason I woke up so different is that I was now truly born again!

Chapter 18   Go To YWAM!

"Religion" held little interest for me. By saying religion I mean standing up, sitting down, playing politics, getting in the right clique at church, reciting prescribed prayers. There is another sense where being religious in terms of being dutiful and repetitive of good things like reading the Bible, going to church, helping the needy, and praying is a good thing but I am talking about motion accomplished in the name of any creed which does not lead to personal contact with the living God. The exciting thing about the new life I had found in Christ however is that from time to time He would speak to me or instruct me what to do.   For example when I had been a Christian for about 8 weeks Jim Moniz told me about a group called Youth With A Mission (YWAM) where you learned to know God then spent 3 months making him known.   Tom Brake lived in a little room upstairs at the Hungry Horse Chapel and I was kneeling by his bed one evening praying and God clearly spoke to me, "Go to YWAM." I replied, "where Lord I hear there are different locations?" He replied, "Hawaii." It was not an audible voice I heard with my ears but God's Spirit speaking to my inner spirit man. Once you are born again your spirit man comes alive and at times there will be a sensing or a knowing or in this case very clear instructions that came from God. (Words this clear have not come to me often.)   I knew God had spoken to me but I wanted to travel the U.S.A. like Dad did when he was 18 so I loaded up my Toyota Pick up with all my carpentry tools and drove to Denver and promptly landed a carpentry job. (I am a hard worker and landing work has never been a problem.) After six weeks I saved enough money to move on so I drove through Colorado Springs to Lake Tahoe Nevada to visit an old party times friend and my B.C. girl Sam. My old friend was always such a fun guy and I enjoyed seeing them and I was trying to shine some light in his world and for Sam. But when they passed the spliff my direction it was hard not to take a hit. And when I saw Sam's luscious form again it made me forget all about Jesus. Day by day I was drifting backwards. I still read my Bible but I also started thumbing through the "Playboys" magazines again. It was a party crash pad and some hot Nevada girls were coming over casting willing eyes on me. As my intimacy with Christ became a dying ember I felt almost suicidal one evening because the new buoyant feeling from my rebirth was starting to be clouded over by lust and weed again.

I had musical ambitions and I was practicing blues harp plenty and becoming good enough to play for money. I arranged to play with a big band at a very large Casino venue. I was getting duded up for the gig and asked God, "shall I do this?" He said "NO." I replied, "I am going to do it anyway." I enjoyed playing music and just wanted to do it. Within 2 to 3 minutes a red rash covered my whole body from my feet clear up to my neck! I told God, "I have reconsidered I won't go play at the club, what do you want me to do anyway?" He replied, "I already told you to go to YWAM in Hawaii you stubborn son of a gun! Now GET GOING!" I replied "Yes Sir!" The joy returned to my insides and I walked upstairs carrying some of my clothes to my pick-up. Sam was up by my truck and she said, "where are you going Buddy?!!" I looked at here with a very animated face and exuded, "I am going to HAWAII !!"
She looked at me with surprise and we said goodbye and I haven't seen her since. I bid my old buddy goodbye too and drove that very night all the way to San Fransisco.

Once there I thought… "well I sure can't drive to Hawaii unless God does a miracle, how am I gonna get there!?" My funds were limited so when I saw musicians playing at the wharf I thought I would try busking. I duded up and played every song I knew through my "Pignose" street amp and finally a lady walked over and gave me $1.00. "Not going to get there doing this," I thought, so I just used the majority of my remaining money for a ticket." I put my truck in storage, bought a ticket for $676.00 and got on my first airplane. People were so nice to me on the plane because they could tell I thought it was pretty dang cool and they liked my story about how God spoke to me to go. But once I arrived I didn't know where to go to get to YWAM so I followed the crowd to Waikiki beach. When I hit the sand and smelled the Plumeria flowers on the moist warm air I thought, "I will never leave here, I have found my paradise!" I didn't have enough money for a room at a hotel so I just slept on a bench at the beach. I was never a bit afraid of people. I always fig-ured most people better be a little afraid of me.

The next day I woke up real early to see the glorious sun-rise on the Pacific and I began walking along the beach. I ran into another young man who seemed ok so we walked and talked along the beach. We sat down on a rock wall absorbing the beauty and then he put his hand on my leg and said, "do you want to get together?" I said, "huh?" He replied, "you know hook up?!" I replied, "you must be one of those faggots!!?" (Croc. Dundee goes to Oahu :) He replied, "well we prefer being called homo-sexuals." I said, "you know the bible talks about how you originally became that way, I read him Romans 1 from my pocket Bible; "God's qualities are clearly seen by looking at the order and beauty of his creation but even though

103

men knew God by observing nature they neither glorified him as God or gave thanks to him, but their thinking became futile and their foolish hearts were darkened. Although they claimed to be wise they became fools and began making statues of men and animals to worship. Therefore God gave them over to their sinful desires and they degraded their bodies with one another. They exchanged the truth of God for a lie and worshipped and served created things instead of the creator. Because of this God gave them over to shameful lusts. Even their women exchanged exchanged natural relations for unnatural ones. In the same way the men also abandoned natural relations with women and were inflamed with lust for one another. Men committed indecent acts with other men, and received in themselves the due penalty for their perversion, Romans 1:21-27 He listened but then said, "no we were born this way as homosexuals." We debated the point a little then parted as friends but not lovers. :) (I realize the term "faggot" is not very politically correct in our era where Obama salutes every gay athlete who goes public but I am just telling my story the way it happened. It just reflects the era, culture, and geography I was raised in and is not meant to insult.)

Enough socializing I needed to learn to surf! I found a cool surfer dude who offered to sell me this hideously ugly tan surf board with so many patches on it that it was more patch than board but the price was only $5.00. Wow! I was so excited! I climbed a very tall Banyon tree about 25 feet and after carefully scoping around, to make sure no one was looking, I hid my wallet in the crotch of the tree. I went out and had a blast getting pushed around by the small waves. So much fun just looking at the beach and the babes! I returned to my tree but when I climbed it my wallet was gone!

I retraced every possible angle of the tree and examined every possible crotch but someone had obviously jacked my wallet! A foreboding feeling came over me as I gathered my belongings for the night. In Hawaii many of the buildings have no windows so I found the nice cafe area of a hotel which had long elegant table clothes that draped down almost to the carpet. I snuck in while no one was watching and slid under the table. I held my breath a little when I saw the shoes of waiters and waitresses walking by real close but that eventually ceased and at about 1:00 AM I drifted off to sleep. When I awoke I looked real carefully under the tables to make sure the shoes were all pointed away from me then emerged. This was my bed for a few days

In 1981 a person didn't just google stuff and I really didn't know where this "YWAM" God told me to go to was and now I was totally broke and my father did an exceptional job at teaching us kids to work so he didn't want to hear any of our problems once we turned 18. So I wasn't quite sure what to do. I just wandered around the beach and I ran into this group reading their bibles in the park. I found out later they were called "The Children of God" I joined their studies and they were really into the word. But when I asked how they ate they just told me; "Man shall not live by bread alone but by every word that proceedeth from the mouth of God." That didn't seem to help me much because I was getting really hungry! Though they didn't give me food they did back a cheap pipe plumb full of choice Hawaiian bud and pass it my way. "Christians who like weed, this really is paradise I thought as I toked up!" Later they showed me how they linger around the dumpster at McDonalds till the old burgers are tossed in...awe finally I had a meal! One of their leaders took a liking to me and we began going around witnessing to people together. There was a form of anointing that would accompany our talks and one time after we talked with a lady we came out of the cafe and someone had left an untouched to go bag with fresh food on the sidewalk. He grabbed it like he expected it and said, "see God provides!" I was pretty blown away but gladly ate the fresh fast food. I also discovered they believed in pre-marital sex which they justified with a verse which said, "to the pure all things are pure." They preached the word on the sidewalks each evening. Had any of their females been attractive to my eyes I may have been even more tempted to join this club!

After a couple days of this I was on the beach alone with my Bible open. I am praying inside, "Lord this group is very dedicated, are they the reason you sent me to Hawaii?" I had since found out YWAM was located on the Big Island which did me a lot of good since I was penniless on Oahu. The day before another gay guy hit on me. I was searching God's word to see if the doctrines I had been hearing were correct when a brown haired guy walked up to me and said, "Hi I am Norm Kurtz I am your older brother in the Lord." I replied, "you are not a homosexual are you?!" He said, "no why do I look like it?" I replied, "no I have just been hit on by them a lot lately." After we visited awhile he told me, "look my friend and I weren't really gelling too well so he and I split up and I would like someone to hang out with." That sounded good to a penniless guy who was eating out of dumpsters so I became his companiero and we hiked and biked and he treated me to a nice crab dinner and a good hotel. He was a very successful businessman from Pennsylvania and he later told me the moment I told him God had told me to come to Hawaii to go to YWAM that God told him, "you make sure and get this guy to YWAM." The only problem now was that I was indoctrinated by the Children of God and was almost persuaded that I was to stay and work with them. So Norm had a delicate job finessing me toward Kona. I had long hair again and had adopted the Children of God custom of not wearing shoes so I was quite a sight hanging out with this rich businessman in posh eateries! He treated me so well and we finally flew out to Kona and made it in the the YWAM office. I just showed up and told them. "God told me to come here and attend your Discipleship Training Program when does it start?" Now the program only started twice a year but they told me, "It starts in two days!" I informed them I had very little money but Norm paid my $100. enrollment fee and they said they would trust God with me for tuition. After I enrolled Norm told me God spoke to His heart that He was supposed to enroll also so he gave someone power of attorney over his enterprises back home and he joined also ! I thought it was pretty amazing that God worked within my stubborn plans to still get me there two days before it started!

At YWAM we enjoyed intelligent speakers who taught us about the loving kind Character of God and how to hear his voice. Others taught us about God's logical and loving limits for sexuality which is marriage. Still others demonstrated the power of God and whole rows of students would fall out of their chairs with some experiencing healing! The worship was awesome and I enjoyed the camaraderie of other students from all over the world; There was Richard, the major drug dealer/ pro-surfer who had recently converted to Christ, some cute girls, and a pro volleyball player from Australia I really enjoyed playing with every afternoon. He told me "James you could have been a pro volleyball player you have great reflexes!" Really Andrew West?! I exclaimed! I always loved sports and learned to love volleyball and soccer.

We learned to know God through our daily quiet time. One day as I was spending time with Christ I asked him, "Lord you took away all my nasty warts since I repented from womanizing but this new wart is growing right on the tip of my index finger and it hurts to play guitar can you please deal with it." I felt an assurance that he would and it got smaller and smaller each day till it was gone! Solid Christians mentored me and one told me, "God doesn't want you smoking pot because he is a jealous God and he wants to fill you with the substance of the Holy Spirit not a drug." He went on to tell me that in the Bible the greek word for drugs is pharmakea and that it means sorcery. The Holy Spirit will not share the temple of your body with sorcery you must take your pick. Having done it as much as I had I agreed that it was like sorcery so instead I opted for the clean holy high the Most High God gives. He also told me, "your body is the temple of the Holy Spirit and God doesn't want you contaminating it with smoke." This brother ran 26 mile marathons and even entered the Ironman Triathlon in Kona so I respected what he said. But they taught me that to avoid going back to that lifestyle I must avoid the people, places, and things which helped me fall back into that rut. When I heeded this advice it proved to be the key to a new start upon my return to Montana.

After 3 months of training my team went to Kauai to make God known in that amazingly beautiful Island. We surfed a good bit at Poi Pu beach on Saturdays and it rained every single day as we prepared skits and music to perform at the huge local flea market. It had rained at least 20 days in a row but the day of our performance not a drop of rain fell! I still had lingering school debt but one day in prayer God told me my Grandma and Aunt would send $1,000.00 so I shouldn't worry. When I received their two cards i opened the first and there was $500.00 !

A van full of mates rejoiced with me and then I declared, "and this envelope will have $500.00 in it also because God said $1,000.00. The van full of YWAMers praised God with me when the word of the Lord proved true!

During my time with YWAM Satan tried to speak to me pretending he was God. I was spending time with God asking him for any special instructions he might have. And I opened my Bible to the beginning page which said, "today _____ and _____ were united in Holy Matrimony" As I viewed the page an inner voice said, "I want you to leave YWAM and go back to Montana and marry _____." That was the blonde I had shot my silver bullet on and had later led to Christ. I ran this new direction by my overseers and they did not feel God would lead me to come there only to change his mind and tell me to leave and go marry someone.. Looking back on it I believe it was a counterfeit word to derail the progress I was now making in Christ. Just as God can give genuine guidance, which is accompanied by peace, joy, and confirmation. The enemy can offer guidance that will take us off course. His guidance is often accompanied by confusion and a sense of "you must do this right now or else!"

Although God has never spoken to me with an audible voice his inner voice was very loud and strong in some of these early leadings probably because I needed it that way in the same way that a parent needs to carefully guide a young child. As I grew more mature in the Lord it seemed he wanted to work together with my own desires and intellect rather than just tell me what to do.

Jeremiah 33:3 says "Call unto me and I will answer you and show you great and mighty things that you know not of." This verse has been instrumental in my life and on several occasions I have woke up at 3:33 AM and God has given me instructions such as when he showed me it was not time to build my 5400 square foot business. YWAM taught us now to know God personally and even to hear his voice.

My time in Hawaii started a lifelong love of boogie boarding which I still really enjoy today ! Even though my first ride at Hapuna beach on a 7 foot wave nearly drowned me us Montana boys get right back on when bucked off !

This is Norm Kurtz after he "rescued" me from the Waikiki beach and took me under his wing to get me to YWAM in Kona. As you can see I had lost weight and was really glad to enjoy the lovely meals he treated me to ! He shares in every soul I have ever won to Christ !

19 Challenging Adjustments (Restitution)

YWAM taught that we should make restitution as much as possible for pre conversion activity that had wronged our fellow man. This was a hard pill for me to swallow because before I came to Christ shoplifting was as natural to me as breathing! I had pilfered local stores for thousands of dollars worth of beef jerky, fishing lures, camping stuff and snacks. I noticed that often, when I stole something, I would lose something I owned that was even nicer. I thought it was Karma. I was good at it so I never got caught but now God had caught me. I really wanted to get right not only with God but with Man so when I came home from YWAM I sold my newer model Toyota Celica sports car. This was one of the nicest rides of my life with a five speed on the floor and awesome cornering capabilities that I pushed to the max on the winding curves of "Going To The Sun" road. I realized the only way for me to pay back all I had stolen was to sell my beloved sports car complete with the new wire spoke rims I had just bought! I did it and went around to many local establishments and just told the owner or manager, "I stole about $250.00 worth of goods from your store but Jesus Christ has recently transformed my life and I want to pay you back and write you a check." Most of them were very grateful and commented that they wish more people would find what I found. A Kalispell sporting goods store was not as gracious. "I think we may want to have you work or do some additional kind of restitution" the manager said. "I will do whatever you feel is right I said because I am guilty," I replied. He came back after a bit and said, "we talked it over and decided it is enough that you came here   to confess and pay for the merchandise." While my Dad and others still scoffed at God's word they were all pretty amazed that this life change even made me sell my sports car and pay everyone back! 111

I experienced a big adjustment of attitude toward law enforcement following my conversion. In the outlaw culture I had become a part of cops were f—ing pigs to be avoided. Now I developed a respect for law enforcement.

YWAM was such an awesome experience living in a community of fun Christ Followers my age but both before YWAM and after returning I dealt with challenging lifestyle adjustments to follow God's way.

There were many many long and lonely Friday and Saturday nights. I used to "Rock and Roll all night" especially on weekends but as a single Christian I often sat home alone trying to keep on the right track because my friends now were often home with their families getting ready for church. One night was especially lonely so I walked down to the Hungry Horse IGA and as I was coming out there was a car full of my favorite friends including Scotty. They shouted, "hey Buddy tonight is senior keggar, we know how you like to party, why don't you join us!" I said, "you guys know I don't do that anymore." One of them shouted, "you are just missing out on life completely aren't you?" I stuck my head inside the window of their car and said with a smile, "I found my life in Jesus!" A grade school friend shouted out from the back seat, "I found my life in the Devil." The others picked up on it and drove off saying, "ya, in the Devil, in the Devil." This buddy had once known the Lord and even witnessed to me some but a week to the day after that night he was coming up US 2 by the water slide on his motorcycle at 1:00 AM and missed the stop sign and was instantly killed when he plowed into the "Mountain Shadows" Motel at 90 m.p.h.. He was a great boxer and a fun kid but it looked to me like he had found his life in the

Devil. After that I talked about God more urgently to some of the guys who were in the car that night and some seemed to listen.

Enduring lonely weekends has not been easy but I know that Heaven and Hell are real and I have reservations for Heaven so I can't get back on the slippery slopes that led to my addictions. I do my best to seek out fellowship but even if I must walk alone I plan on sitting at the marriage supper of the lamb. My

good friend Don Downing (above with niece Leslie) was a famous bar fighter who had come to know Christ. He drove a D-8 Cat on highway jobs. One time he was far from home driving Cat and the girls on his job kept inviting him to come to the bar even to just drink a 7-Up and socialize. He was about to cave in and go one night when a tough look-ing 165 pound man appeared in his camper trailer. Don told me he had a knock down drag out fight with the dude for a long time and ripped up the inside of the trailer! He said he had unusual strength and that it was a helluva fight. Finally Don got the advantage and with all his might shouted "you'll never get me Satan!" and with that Don broke the man's arm and when he did the man disappeared. I retorted, "Are you sure it wasn't just a dream or a vision Don?!" "No James, it was a real man and a real fight!" Since Don was one of the most famous bar fighters our region ever produced I had to believe him. Even for those of us who fight only in the invisible world I find that the fight is also real when it comes to resisting temptation and staying on God's path. Since I was so wild before conversion I didn't always feel like I fit in with the church crowd. But Don and I became good friends because we were cut from the same mold Let me take a rabbit trail and tell you how he came to Christ: Don had never lost a bar fight that anyone of us knew of and was also undefeated as an arm wrestler. He was a hard working man but a hopeless alcoholic. Drunk Don got so angry one day that he went down to where his son Jim and Mike were playing softball and challenged the whole team to a fight. He felt so disgusted with himself after that that he grabbed his rifle and started driving up the North Fork to end his life. But his car broke down right in front of The Hungry Horse Chapel. He looked up and saw a little white cross then went in the doors where Don Ferko was conducting a revival service. He didn't even sit down but walked straight up to the altar and said, "Preacher I need help!" They led him to Jesus, wiped the blood off his face, and he came out of the church that night never needing another drink of alcohol for the rest of his days! He and I were good friends till he went home to be with the Lord. Many people in our region called him "Uncle Don" because he was a big hearted Democrat who helped many people who were down on their luck. I am not saying God is against every believer doing some social drinking and mingling on a Saturday night but I never forgot Don telling of how he wrestled Satan over social drinking so I have opted to quit both partying and the party scene. Though I struggle very little now with alcohol or drugs i still must keep my distance from hot looking drunk girls with jiggling boobs.

I looked as wild as I was before coming to Christ. My long hair felt real nice on my shoulders and I loved to snap my neck forward then back to whip it into place. My hero was Wild Bill Hickock and I was lightning fast with my Colt revolver. Martin City was and is a rather outlaw town and I often wore my iron strapped to my leg like some of the other wild west characters who inhabit The Deer Lick Bar,

The Packers Roost, or Scotty's Dad's club; The South Fork Saloon. I wore a faded Levi jacket that was so old it was coming apart at the seams. But I had used buckskin to tie the seams together. The bottom to this two piece suit were well broken in 501 jeans with no underwear! (My Christian Friend Tom later had a talk with me that I should wear underwear LOL!.)

 But my new Christian friends all had short hair and most of them dressed like dorks so soon I found myself cutting my hair and wearing clean cut clothes like them just to fit in. God didn't tell me to do this but I guess it was naturally conforming to new peer pressure. Looking back I think I should have kept some of the outer trappings of my former life because I could have reached more of my old friends had I retained more of my cultural swag. Some people don't reject Jesus but reject the culture we represent. I was an insider in the hard partying up the line mountain boys and could have impacted more lives had I just been myself in a Christian form. Jesus set free a demoniac and the guy wanted to join Jesus and the disciples but Jesus told him.."no just go back to your friends and family and tell them what I have done for you." If someone had told me that I could have reached people that wouldn't listen to outsiders.

Probably the biggest mistake that I made was changing my name from "Buddy" to James. When I was three my sister Jamey couldn't say "brother" and began calling me her "little bruddy." The name changed to Buddy and by the time I was six the only name people knew me by was Buddy or Bud. After being a little famous from baseball and notorious for partying the whole valley knew me by that name. But in my zeal to please God I thought I should change my name from Buddy to my God given name James. My thinking was that Buddy

115

was a slime ball so now I should have a new name to go with my new born again persona. It was a noble thought I guess but it really turned off plenty of my old mates and in some ways minimized the impact of my conversion. Some of my old mates would sneeringly call me "JAAM-MEESS" in a formal sounding mocking voice. But maybe it was good that my name change made me odious to some of my former friends because even though Christ had taken away the inner urge for drugs and alcohol if I had kept hanging with my friends I may have fallen back into the same familiar ruts. After I wouldn't let anyone call me Buddy for six months and made people call me James I actually realized that James sounded a little too formal to even me and I missed the friendly sounding ring of the name Buddy.

In retrospect I think with much of the change God brings in our lives we can easily add to the genuine article with religious junk that God has nothing to do with. Jesus is after the heart not necessarily the culture. Surfers, hipsters and rappers have become disciples of Christ but held onto their B.C. culture and reached more people. But with my conversion I changed my culture too quickly and in some cases added man made baggage to the genuine work God had done in my life. That is also what happened in Jesus day; a group called the Pharisees had taken good rules God had given, such as resting and worshipping on one day of the week, and had added as many as 496 legalistic crazy religious no no's to further define what God originally intended. By the time they were done adding their man made no no's to God's law Jesus rebuked them saying, "You experts in the law, woe to you, because you load people down with burdens they can hardly carry. And you yourselves will not lift one finger to help them" Luke 11:46 He even called them blind

116

guides!" Jesus got so pissed at religious people who just made up more bondage trips to place on their fellow man but would not lift a finger to help them. On the other hand He bid us "Come to me, all you who are weary and burdened, and I will give you rest. Take my yoke upon you and learn from me, for I am gentle and humble in heart and you will find rest for your souls. For my yoke is easy and my burden is light." Matthew 11:28-30 If you have been bitterly disappointed with religion you are a good candidate to come to Christ and find rest for you soul. If your God thing makes you burdened you need to switch brands and pick up the burden light brand of Christ's true teaching! Keep it simple and realize God loves you and you should love others. I enjoy a simple phrase I gleaned from Brian Houston; "Love God, Love Life, and Love People!"

I too have been greatly let down by "religion". Once I started a church and grew it for one and a half years and my overseers asked me to give the work, the money, the chairs, the people to a more experienced pastor saying that I would be the assistant pastor.   But as soon as I signed everything over they just said, "bye James." It was as though I had never existed. Perhaps you also have been stung by religion but I encourage you to not let go of the lover of your soul and to change churches if you must but stay plugged in to a Christian assembly. Though Jesus despised religious dogma that really hindered people even he was always in church every Saturday.

The Prince of Darkness was angry that the prayers of God's people had intersected with a divine destiny on my life enough to give spiritual birth to a well known party

animal. Once he couldn't keep me from the light he immediately tried to bring false light my way. In 17 years of
living in darkness no Mormon or Jehovah's Witness had
ever talked to me but within a few days of my coming to
Jesus both Mormon's and J.W.'s showed up on my step
to convince me of their doctrines and give me literature.
Thank God for wise friends who showed me how their
doctrines deviate from a solid understanding of who Jesus is. The Bible calls Satan the deceiver who will appear
not as a wicked red devil but as a smooth talking religion
that doesn't believe that Jesus is God Almighty, The Son
of God, and the author and finisher of our salvation. Paul
said in Galations if anyone comes to you and brings another new and improved gospel let him be eternally
condemned. Satan did his best to deceive me with false
cults like Mormonism, Jehovah's Witness, or The Children of God but my habit of staying plugged in to a true
Christian church kept me on track. (Make sure whatever
group you join believes that the Bible is God's Word and
believes in the Trinity and basic clean living.)

A storm of persecution came my way from my Father.
God's Spirit on me made me bold and I boldly witnessed
to him but he was by nature very bold and very loud in
what he believed. For about 10 days Dad was extremely
grateful that whatever had happened to me took me off
drugs and alcohol but once I began telling him who it was
that freed me the sparks began to fly! I remember before
going to Bible School I was in his employ and he literally
took 2 to 3 hours each day to scream at me about how
stupid I was to believe in the Bible and how Jesus was
just another man! He would go on and on about how sci-
ence has thoroughly proved we evolved and that

believing in a creator God was just lunacy. I needed the money I was making to go to Bible school though so I just put up with it and did my work. Dad and I always loved each other at the core however and I still admire the great fearless man that he was who taught me to do carpentry at a young age and stuck with my Mom even when she was paralyzed.

 Later in life I performed Dad's second marriage where at age 81 he married an 83 year old Jewess. His second wife was the only person we ever knew who could stand up to him in a yelling match! She loved Jesus and gave Dad a constant earful. Though he persecuted me very strongly at first I was always very close to Dad and loved his fun loving personality. He attended my church when he was in town but to my knowledge never fully accepted Christ. He could never deny the great work God had done in my life though. One time after I had been sharing my life with Dad and his second wife Gladys. I heard them talking in the bedroom afterwards. Gladys said,

"Jim, is it really true that James was so wild before he knew Christ?" *Dad replied, "He wasn't just a wild Indian, he was completely off the reservation!"*

Dad with my daughter Esther.

119

20 How Jesus Became Real to me

My first remembrance of feeling the presence of God was when I was 5 years old. Someone had taught me the song; "Jesus Loves Me This I Know." I was walking across an abandoned barn-wood foundation in our back yard and I began singing that song and a feeling that God was near and did love me came over me. Something like a clean loving feeling. But then it went away. I think we are all born with a sensitivity to good and evil. Perhaps we even have an inward ability to sense God and sense when we are crossing over into evil. I felt that but I kept violating that still small voice. At age six I shot a sparrow with my BB gun. At first I felt bad for terminating its life for no reason but after I shot a few more sparrows it was just a part of life. Funny how the Bible says Jesus knows when even a sparrow falls to the ground…. Jesus was busy counting when our neighborhood gang got our guns out!

 I had an unusual fascination with the female body and by the time I was seven I had "Playboy" magazines in my backyard fort. What beauty! Most of us hoodlums had similar stashes. The nice feeling of that Jesus song kind of got crowded out by the stash in my back fort.

The first time I shoplifted was to get my Dad a real good present for Father's Day. I stole a nice pen holder with a duck on it. I was shaking the first time I stole. But eventually I did it so routinely that it was just part of my day. I never got caught, I was a clever kid. But one time Bobby and I stole some big stuff from the B&B but when Bob exited the store after me the clerk ran out and grabbed him. Bob was pretty tough and wheeled around and kicked the clerk in the groin and ran off. That was the closest we ever came to getting caught.

In the beginning our conscience is tender but as we vio-late it more and more we become hard. In the beginning I trembled while shoplifting now everywhere I went i stuck stuff in my coat. I had once felt weird about getting naked with a girl and crossing lines but after awhile i felt it was morally fine to do so. My conscience became seared and my heart became hard.

I was so hard by the time I was 16 that the night my own mother died I dropped some acid, drank some beer, and got really crazy in "The Little Green Buger." That night when the passing lane was clogged I passed a string of cars through the right hand ditch going about 60 mph through the gravel narrowly missing reflectors and wheel-ing up wildly back onto the pavement in front of the horri-fied honking motorists! Later that night I got busted when Police raided the keggar I was at and I had to spend some time at the jail.

But how does a person that was as hard as I was; a per-son who never went to church, a person who was com-pletely convinced of Darwinism and talked others out of their faith, a person who would sometimes persuade Christians to get stoned with me, a person who was "running with the Devil", as Eddie Van Halen would say, for years. How does a person as hard as I was ever come to true faith in Christ?

For me it took Jesus Christ becoming much more than a story in a book. For me God became a tough, relevant unseen force that came into my world uninvited and wouldn't let up till I bowed my knee to his supremacy.

To do that he had to cut through my stereotypes of Christians. The Christian kids I knew were no good in a fight so I didn't respect them. I bullied them and took away their candy on Halloween and they didn't even have enough balls to resist. The only real contact with Christianity that I had was that there was two old ladies who got out their flannel-graphs and put these gay looking pictures of Jesus and his buddies on the board and if we sat through the boring deal we got candy at lunch hour in school. To me it was hogwash. Just some fables old ladies who didn't know about evolution made up to make themselves feel better when they died. The few Christians I did know seemed happy enough but I always thought that they just didn't know how fun sex, fighting, and drugs were so they just kind of enjoyed the naive little boring truths they had found refuge in. I talked more than one Christian into jumping off the bandwagon and enjoying some Pot with me.

But Grandma and Mom were praying for me and now and then the light brought on by their prayers would pierce the darkness. The first encounter came when I had broken my leg real bad in the accident I described. After over a month in the hospital they finally let me go home and one night I had a dream in which the doctor told me I had twenty four hours to live. I got with my best friends and went skiing and did the things I enjoyed most then the end of the 24 hour period drew near and I prepared myself to die. In the dream my sister Jamey came by and said, "Bud you cannot die till you first call on Jesus!" I said "Ok." So I picked up the old circular dial phone we had and dialed J - E - S- U- S. Right after I did it I died. In the dream my spirit detached itself from my body and I rose up over my dead body. I looked down on it like one might look upon a scene from a rising silent helicopter. I was totally at peace and knew Jesus had made everything all right after I called on Him. I awoke and thought, "that was a cool dream I think I will go to church sometime." I found out it was Sunday.... Easter Sunday. My paralyzed Mom would hobble two blocks to "The Hungry Horse Chapel." I walked with her that morning. The Hungry Horse Chapel was a dying church till this beamy eyed fanatic named Jack MacDonald came and they got real wild in that church. They would scream and raise their hands and speak in tongues and march around in circles and the church started to grow. Us neighborhood hoodlums thought it was funny and some-times we would get stoned and go in to the service just to make fun of them. Or to pretend we were getting wild too! On more than one occasion I stayed in the church to make sure no one left while my buddy would siphon gas out of the cars in the parking lot. Well this day was different. I was not going to make fun of them or to si-phon gas I was going to find out about the Jesus I met in the dream. The bearded song leader started to singing "I saw the light, I saw the light, no more darkness, no more night, now I'm so happy no sorrow in sight, praise the Lord! I saw the Light!" As I joined in the singing I could feel a clean life giving presence coming into my tired hard soul. I literally walked out of the church singing the song and along came my partying buddy Eddie Whitaker out in front of the church. We got together and within an hour we were drinking some "Black Velvet" and I totally forgot about my spiritual encounter for another couple of years. (The Bible says Satan comes immediately to steal the word sown in the seeking heart lest the word take root and produce lasting change. That is what happened to me.) I wish I had continued in the faith then and I would have spared myself from getting STD's and other hard-ships but no one took me under their wing and taught me how to do it. Then again maybe I had to bottom out a lit-tle more till I was thoroughly sick of the life I was living. Till I, like the prodigal son, had spent all I had and squandered my mental and physical assets until I was was feeding the pigs/demons.   *Note: Eddie gave his life to Christ years later and now we both serve God!

I found out later that the Church was going to close but a godly man named Lloyd Fine went up in the prayer room and cried out to God, "You must have some man some where who is not concerned about money and numbers who will come here to be the pastor!?" God answered his prayer and Pastor Jack came and ushered in a move of God. I think one of the keys was that the church kept a prayer room and often there was somebody in the prayer room praying. Unfortunately Pastor MacDonald committed adultery with the song leaders wife and the growing crowd was shocked but now it was a congregation that could attract a Pastor and a young pastor named George Moore came out of Bible college and took the church. My mother was a member and had made a substantial land contribution which the new sanctuary of that church sits on to this day.   I think the praying church was praying for Laverne's crazy kid Buddy.

Jesus said to know him we must become like little children. I think that means we must get that sensitivity of conscience and tender intuitive friendship with God back. That happened to me when I got born again in the fashion I previously described.

Chapter 21 What happened with the fighter in me?

After becoming a Christian I was talking to my brother in law Rob Quist and he said he never had to get in a fight. This dumbfounded me because to me fighting was an inescapable part of life. I grew up knowing my Dad fought plenty and everyone in Hungry Horse elementary had to fight. But to my amazement I read in the Bible where Jesus said, "If someone strikes you on the one cheek turn to him the other one also." After adopting his peace loving ways I never had to get in another fight! I even got tested on that verse once. My friend Mark Barnes and I were witnessing on the street in Kona, Hawaii. We were talking with a 6 foot 4 inch black man that must have weighed 285. He sold hats and had at least six stacked on his head. He told us, "all you need is love....then he played a few notes on his flute." I said something along this line; The Bible declares that you don't even know true love until Jesus comes into your heart and infuses you with the Love of the Father. At that he punched/ slapped me right in the face. I didn't strike back. Then my friend Mark put his face up to him and said, "That wasn't very loving!" So he slapped Mark hard too! Mark and I went away feeling glad because we thought we were being persecuted for a worthy cause. I don't know if we were hit for Christ or hit for boldness but I noticed I didn't hit back like I used to. The Bible says we were "children of wrath" before God's Spirit made us alive in Christ. Indeed before you and I receive a heart change we are children of wrath and arrogance and fighting seems almost unavoidable. Before I knew Christ I was full of anger and would regularly hit my dash and sometimes doors or a wall. But when Christ came into my life I became comparatively peaceful.

I even became a peacemaker once when I was witnessing on the streets of Anchorage, Alaska. I was telling a young hoodlum my testimony and two female wildcats came roaring out of the bar with broken off beer bottles in their hands about to tear each other apart. The hoodlum asked me, "aren't Christians supposed to be peacemakers?!" I said, "ya". He said, "Then why don't you go stop that fight?" I said, "why don't you help me and we'll do it." He said, "OK." So he and I waded in between them and stopped it!

The only time I have had to put up my dukes as a believer was when I was coming home late at night in Yaroslavl Russia in 1992. After finishing teaching about 150 young people God's word we were sauntering down a lonely street on the way to our apartment when two cocky thugs blocked our path and demanded our money. My partner rebuked them in the name of Jesus and I put up my dukes like a guy who knew how to use them and they backed off and let us proceed!

A rather strange thing happened though with my fighting instinct. God turned me into a spiritual warrior. He took the fighting resolve that would not run even when my friends did on the night to remember and turned that into a strong resolve to fight for the gospel, to fight for His Church, to fight against darkness. On my baseball team I had a Derek Jeter like reputation for never missing a game no matter what shape I was in and God has used that same perseverance to make me not back down even when all hell and wicked people are trying to stop my meetings. (And I have had stubborn demon inspired people try to stop my meetings in several continents.) The only time there was absolutely no way to proceed and I had a meeting stopped was in India last month when

126

160 militant anti-Christians surrounded our crusade grounds on their motorcycles and started tearing stuff up and threatening to harm me and tear the place up if I so much as entered the arena. A great crowd of about 3,000 people were filtering into the crusade grounds for the meeting so I didn't want to let them stop us! I insisted my host Dr. Daya Dayanandam take me as close as he dared. I could tell he was scared as we ventured to within about 6 blocks from the crusade grounds. He pointed out a square littered with hundreds of flowers where the venue protesters had engaged in a flower ceremony to empower their venomous outrage. I thought of just going in regardless of the consequences but then the 6 host pastors inside the grounds informed me that the 25 police present strictly forbade us to continue because of the obvious violence that was erupting. At that point I gave up for the first time in my life but it is probably good I did because the next day we discovered that the militants had piled up a bunch of rocks in an upper tier that they planned to stone me with had I taken the stage. The next day my scheduled devotion read "From the sovereign Lord comes escape from death." Dr. Daya and I visited the mountain where the Lord's apostle doubting Thomas was speared in the city of Chennai the next day and I had to wonder if those same Christ hating spirits were still in operation. (But God wonderfully worked through the martyrdom of Thomas as today Chennai has more churches and Christians than anywhere else in India!)

The Jesus I came to know was not a weak willed wimp walking around in a sheet saying "peace brother". The Jesus I came to know was a rough tough carpenter who came to make us strong, free, manly, and resolute. I never perceived him as one who came to make me less of a man than I was before but more of a man. That is why I have done many gutsy things as a believer including work 22 hours a day as a commercial fisherman based out of Kodiak, Alaska. Hunt Elk with a navy seal who keeps a pretty good pace, train with the MMA fighters in Manila, and go boldly into countries that were at war to preach the gospel.

Sure we need a tenderness in relationships and in nurturing the weak sheep but I like dudes in the Bible like king David and his mighty men. I see Jesus as the Lion of the Tribe of Judah not as the wuss from the Catholic church. I relate to John G. Lake who preached "The Strong Man's Gospel" Lake believed Jesus came to make us strong men who could even defeat the power of sickness and Satan.

This theological bent of mine contrasts sharply with the "less of me and more of thee"…. "I become a worm so you can be my all in all" philosophy of much of the Church but that's ok Jesus theology contrasted sharply with his religious contemporaries also.

So in terms of what God did with my fight I think he redirected it away from people and toward fighting demonic strongholds. At two key times of spritual struggle my wife and once my kids also witnessed me stand up on my bed while I was asleep and start pulverizing the wall like I was Mike Tyson in the ring! I was boxing in my sleep against spiritual enemies. I had to patch my wall and my knuckles afterwards. Still a warrior but now one who fasts and prays and speaks words of faith. I was invited to hold numerous meetings in Russia while the U.S.A. was bombing Bosnia. Even my courageous host Brad Hansen asked me if I really wanted to come because the train station in one of our cities had been bombed by Muslim rebels. I was having second thoughts after Brad told me that but that night a powerful white angel that looked like Mel Gibson in "Braveheart" appeared to me and I knew I would be OK! An angry Russian did try to pick a fight with me on a bus in Moscow but I persevered and we had very powerful meetings! In fact I got to sing and testify on television because the city was amazed I had come at a time when Russia was inflamed with anger against Americans!

On another occasion Jaekyung and i decided to preach the gospel in a dangerous slum in Montego Bay Jamaica. Numerous locals urged us to not go in to the Gulley Ghetto but we kept walking… then a local called out from a window, "Don't go in there they will chew you up and spit you out dead!" I replied "no they won't they will never get past my angels!" Not only did we go in but we established a church in the ghetto! So God took my fighting instinct and redirected it into fighting for lost souls.

I still find myself toying with the idea of doing some actual fighting again however. I am a few weeks away from being 52 but I am a fitness fanatic who loves the gym and I could still get in the ring I think. I am not sure it would be wise to do so at this age but I did train in an MMA gym twice in Manila. Right now I am doing construction all day with a 5 pound nail gun and am in good shape! Maybe my next book will be about my comeback! Ha Ha!

Looking at Playboy or Penthouse magazine had become an almost nightly habit for me but when Jesus came into my life I didn't even feel like looking at my porn magazines at night for a few days. And instead of following the girls in the hallway at school like a buck in rut I felt pure and holy for about 3 days! At first I thought I would never have another impure thought and it would be gone just like the inner drive for drugs and alcohol was but soon I found myself just as horny as before. I missed Sam my girlfriend so badly. I so missed her perfect boobs. Saved or not I missed these delightful perfect playthings! So I invited her to church real nice and tried to tell her how wonderful it would be to have God in her life. She finally let me know that she didn't want to go to church, give her life to Jesus, or quit partying so we drifted apart. The hardest thing to give up was my girlfriend...she was SO HOT even though I never felt she was truly mine alone. Somehow I got over giving up Sam and I didn't even have a girlfriend or didn't even kiss a girl for 7 years after I got saved.   (There were nights before I got saved that I kissed more than one in a night but now I went seven years without even kissing one!) I still don't know how I did it. I just felt that I had messed that whole area of my life up so thoroughly that I needed some kind of cleansing wherein I would seek first the Kingdom of God and taste a little purity.   One time I was driving by the Deer Lick Saloon and Dawn came out and laid a big uninvited smooch on my lips but I just wiped it off and tried to tell her some more about Jesus! She eventually got saved and quit being one of the canyon's worst teen alcoholics.

  It was not easy for me to keep away from girls for 7 years... it was often a daily struggle to not go back to enjoying the fun that was once such a part of my life. But

Jesus said the way was narrow that led to life and few would find it and I was determined to be one of the few. God didn't necessarily ask me to do that but frankly I was used to some pretty hot girls and I didn't find the looks of any of the Christian girls I now met that appealing so I just focused on growing in my new faith till I would find a Christian girl I was genuinely attracted to,

In YWAM we had the privilege of having intellectual lucid speakers give great practical instruction on a wide variety of Christian living including sexuality. One of their great talks was "God's logical and loving limits" wherein they explained that when we have sex we become one with that other person. This oneness is meant to be protected and preserved through marriage. Yet today many become one then jerk apart which often leaves them as somewhat fragmented people. They explained that sex is God's idea, the devil didn't think it up, but since the creator made it he also gave an owners manual which provided logical and loving limits for the proper usage and fullest enjoyment of this amazing gift.

After hearing this teaching I realized why I still felt empty even though I had been sleeping with a 10. I also felt an unusual amount of compassion for the girls I had used rather than truly loved. I declared a fast for them and prayed sincerely for those I had laid. After awhile one little blonde I knew intimately told me that she had just experienced about two serious car wrecks in the last ten days. I told Cathy that life was probably trying to get her attention so she could look heaven ward like I had. She really listened and I was able to share how much God loved her and how meaningful her life could be with Jesus in her heart. She responded by saying "Buddy your eyes are glowing so powerfully (the glow was from the Holy Spirit) and yes I need to say that prayer… I could have died in the wreck." After praying to receive Christ her eyes were filled with a glow I had never seen in them before. I thought that was pretty cool! Once we were just "workin' on our night moves" and now we were both glowing like bulbs with the Holy Spirit! We had much fun as buddies in the Lord and I helped her get established as a new Christian. She later wanted to turn our relationship back into "more than friends" but I just didn't have that in my heart for her so she married someone else but was still serving God the last time I checked on her.

I had love interests in that seven year purification period and dealt regularly with lust issues but somehow I was pretty on fire for God and was keeping it under wraps on a daily basis.

When I was about 25 I got back into cross country ski racing. I was no longer an Olympic hopeful but enjoyed it and did ok even winning one race. I got my friend Dale Lee into racing also and we attended a race in central Montana. At the race I noticed a smoking hot Norwegian blonde racer who looked amazing in her tight white racing suit. We had caught each others eye at the meet and in the evening we met at the hostel many of us racers were staying in. She sat talking with me in her ripped up sexy jeans. After talking for a long time the old me really wanted to take the next step but I resisted because I wanted to please God and didn't know what my Christian friend would think if I ditched him to disappear in the back room with this hottie! Part of me was really regretting not going further than I did with this amazing girl who seemed to like me. So on the way home I asked my my friend Dale, "Dale what is wrong with two people who both want to to enjoy each others body doing so outside of marriage?" He gave me a great answer, "James every time you exercise self control you are purchasing assurance for your future bride that you will be a worthy husband which she won't have to be constantly worrying about in terms of what you might be doing while she is away."

After I got some of the adventures out of my system that I knew I could probably only pull off as a single dude, such as commercial fishing in Alaska, I fasted and told God, "God I can't take this sexless single gig ANY MORE! Your word says if we ask for a fish you won't give us a snake. I ask for a girl that will help me love you more and we can serve you together and God she has to be at least an 8." (I didn't hear Christians do this much but as a worldly guys we rated girls on a scale of one to ten. The one I gave up for God was a ten in my and others opinions)

I had a few dates with a nice Christian girl I was only mildly interested in and my sister introduced me to a hot blonde that couldn't seem to take her eyes off me and my eyes were kind of glued on her too. But I knew God told his followers not to be unequally yoked with an unbeliever so the disciple in me pressed the over-ride button on the fleshly me that just wanted to go for it with this cute girl. (I am glad I did, later someone told me she had been to bed with 19 guys and I could have ended up just being another notch on her belt!)

The answer I was praying for didn't come immediately but God had told me to go to Uganda so I signed up to serve at the new YWAM base in Jinja, Uganda. I envisioned myself single forever if I served God in Africa so

before going my sister Bonni and I took a trip all over Europe and I we stayed at many YWAM bases so I could scope out the prospects! Bon lectured me that I came off disinterested in girls and that I might never marry unless I loosened up. I retorted, "I am just looking for the right one and am not going to lead others on till I find her."
  Even my worldly friends would get mad at me some Saturday nights because I was always pretty picky and wouldn't chase someone I wasn't interested in. As our "Euro-rail" train pass wound down to the final days Bon went to Spain and I went to Sweden to the YWAM base there to see if any Christians were cute in a country that had proved a mother lode of cute girls in my days as a skier. None were... maybe hot looking girls just have so much temptation from the world that it is very hard for them to serve God but all the hot babes were on the streets of Stockholm not in the YWAM base. (Though I have seen other bases with cute girls.) Some of you are probably thinking I place too much emphasis on outward appearance but the truth is I know myself and since for most Christian marriage is a one and done kind of deal I wanted to find that rare combination of character and beauty. I never pictured myself marrying an African girl so I really felt doomed when I got on the plane for Africa because I heard there was only one elderly nurse at the YWAM base in Uganda. But the first day I arrived at the Kenya base a herd of cows came onto the mission compound's lawn. Nobody knew what to do but being from Montana I gave a good whoop and chased them off! Coming back from chasing the cows I found something better to chase; a cute Korean girl that struck me as a girl of good character and we talked. We spent more time over the next few days and God spoke to my Spirit, "this will be your wife." She then went to Europe and I to Uganda but later she returned and we dated more.

I thought she was cute enough to marry but then when we dated she wore a low cut dress and I was pretty floored by her chest! She was asking me what my spiritual vision was and all I could do was try to remember my name! We got married and were blessed with 3 awesome kids.

We enjoyed years of good marriage and great sex and I was so very thankful for God's gift of a cute Christian wife. For the most part the first 20 years of marriage was great but sometimes the memories of the different hot experiences I had were hard to get over even in marriage. Having eaten from a smorgasbord made the good meal of Christian marriage somewhat bland at times. I found myself wishing I had never ruined my taste buds with forbidden fruits. Years of porn use as an unbeliever also made being an upright Christian man much, much harder. Many times it seemed like I had to keep on the straight and narrow path one day at a time and with my jaw set like a flint. I wondered why God had delivered me from the appetite for drugs and alcohol but I still dealt with real temptations and inner conflict.

God guided me to my first wife Jaekyung after 7 years of me giving up girls as I pursued Jesus and His Kingdom

Chapter 23   Dealing With My Achilles Heal

Maybe it was because God designed in us an appetite for sex while the drugs and alcohol were not really by design meant for us to abuse. Problem was I was fighting some of my same addictive tendencies but now in the realm of sex/porn/ meeting girls I was crazy about but now couldn't have sex with because I was a Christian.   Maybe God left this for me to struggle with just so I would be dependent on him for mercy and would not become a judgmental type Christian who looked down on those who struggled but with a different sin than mine. I think there are areas we should stand against governmentally; using abortion as birth control, making gay marriage the cultural normative standard, legalizing drugs that are not healthy for society.... but its never to be confused with not being loving and merciful to people who are sinners like us but with a different sin than "our Achilles Heal."

  My sin was receiving my formative training from Hugh Hefner so that I viewed girls partly as "Playmates" rather than "I'm gonna grow up and marry one someday."

Before God released the chain of events that led to my first marriage I did a several day fast that I think he was using to get my old thoughts out of my system. But even after marriage Crazy temptations came my direction to try to get me to fall;   I accompanied the youth group to a multi-day Christian concert and the girl which many considered the hottest blonde cheer-leader in the high school was forcefully pulling her eyes away from me the whole trip and then finally looked right in my eyes with her beautiful blue eyes and said, "geez its too bad you are already taken!" I was probably 35 at the time and hate to admit that I was miserably tested inside and hoping to bend scripture to accommodate her interests but I didn't encourage anything as I was a leader. Another rough temptation was when I did concerts in Russia and a 21 year old Christian knock-out fell for me and sat right next to me at every possible chance she could get. She could have been on the cover of major magazines yet she was fun and loved the Lord and loved me. Even though I never took action toward her affection it took me about two months to get her face out of my minds eye after I came home from that trip. I struggled with feeling a capacity to love more than one girl. Maybe it was just that I am not a guy who should stay away from my wife. But even with my wife I had girls hit on me;

Another time I was out witnessing with my wife in Jamaica and a young hottie came up to me and said in a breathy voice, "I liiikkkeee you! Let's meet somewhere together, we can keep it secret you know." That wasn't as hard to resist because because I knew it was the devil trying to keep me from witnessing to people about Christ. But since this has been my major area of weakness the enemy kept hitting me where I was most vulnerable. Maybe some of it was that my hobby is fitness and weight-lifting and some gals just like the way I look but especially knowing what I would have done in those situations before being a believer made it hard. I was born again but not dead and buried !

Then came the internet and the abundance of temptation it represented. I didn't want it in our house but my wife and kids did so I installed preventative software and took other measures but fell every few months into porn even though I was a pastor. I didn't touch another girl physically in 24 years of marriage but the time to time porn was adultery of a different sort that was probably a quiet cancer in my marriage.

I don't know why this area has been such an ongoing struggle for me.   My counsellor thinks I may have tweaked my developmental template by exposing myself to porn from the 3rd grade. He explained that our brain is ready to take certain things in at a certain age and when a kid like me views porn in grade school it can have a warping effect - maybe I needed that seven year period of celibacy I spoke of earlier for God to restore the factory preset settings on me so I could enjoy the real 3-D live partner experience he was getting ready to provide and not be stuck on my 2-D porn turn ons !   I realize many marriages deal with the issue of porn; some even watch together to spice things up, others fight sex addiction in one partner as a mutual battle. But my wife was such a good virgin girl from an almost perfect family who thought she married a missionary and was pretty blown away by the real things I dealt with as an x party animal. If I did open up sometime she looked at me like she had mistakenly drawn the lottery ticket to marry "Jack the Ripper!" I thank God that my second wife Mary has a lot more grace for this area because I think she feels its a natural temptation that she is not totally above even herself.

A man once asked Kenneth E. Hagan, "pray that I will not have all these temptations any more!" The man of God replied, "Ok I will pray that you die!" It wasn't what the man wanted to hear but the pastor explained that while we live in this earth suit we will deal with temptation. But the more accurate prayer is, "deliver us from temptation." (I heard he said the sex at eighty with his wife was better than earlier in their marriage.)

Paul told the Corinthian believers "if you burn with lust get a wife or husband and fulfill each others need."

For me the best cure to this area of weakness was marriage. Thank God that he gave me a lovely attractive Korean wife and the mother of my 3 kids; named Jaekyung. She is a devoted servant of God, a gifted kids minister, an excellent mother, and we had a good marriage for about 20 years and were used of God in many nations of the world! And thank God that he had mercy on the still a little crazy Buddy Willows when I couldn't totally make the first marriage go the distance !

Neither Jaekyung nor I committed adultery and both remained faithful in our Christian walk. But our lives and interests grew in different directions with me needing help at my business and her sick and tired of it and missing her white collar past. There were also huge differences in how to raise kids as my upbringing involved being taught how to work and working even as a six year old and hers involved total parental support and only study till she graduated from college. Throw that in the mix as a relational time bomb ! LOL !

After 20 good years I stayed in it for the kids for about 3 and neither of us was very happy or content. The University of Texas offered her a full ride Masters degree program that included a large monthly stipend in Austin and I was feeling a need for companionship and help in Montana and after the longest physical separation of our marriage, which I objected to but her pastor insisted on, things came to a head and she served me papers. I didn't fight it much because we had had about 20 counseling sessions but it had gotten worse not better. Yes God hates divorce but the Bible also says it is better to sleep on the corner of a roof than with an ill content complaining wife - or for that matter an ill content complaining husband. She felt unloved and I felt disrespected and unappreciated and we couldn't manage to work our way out of it.

A pastor I admire named Fred Price says he keeps his wife with him everywhere he preaches. He says "why open myself up to temptation when God has provided a safe harbor for me." Had we heeded that advice our marriage may still be in tact but the unfortunate reality is it is not and attempts at reconciliation failed. We both own the demise of our marriage equally. (But going forward I just keep Mary with me instead of doing concerts in a country for two weeks without my wife like before.)

Divorce was harder than I thought it would be both for me personally and for our kids. It was like going through an earthquake for all of us. With most of our closest friends just watching from the sidelines, some throwing out caustic condemnation, and others kind of washing their hands of us in a way. I have a deep respect for Jaekyung and still honor her years of waging spiritual warfare to bring forth God's Kingdom together with me. I fasted and prayed at least twenty times for my family and often after the fasts Jaekyung would for some reason call me but it was never with a real desire to do the hard work of getting into intensive counseling to mend fences so I eventually remarried.

During the single years after my divorce my weakness was more pronounced without a wife and it drove me to a great Christian ministry called Celebrate Recovery. This ministry is devoted to helping people overcome hurts, habits, and hangups. They would give out chips for "periods of sobriety:" I had quite a few 30 and 60 day chips for not looking at porn but needed remarriage to get to the one year and two year chips. But it was nice to have others with me to "celebrate my recovery."

Through this group I have learned tools to overcome porn and lust. One tool is an acronym called H. A. L. T. I learned if I am hungry, angry, lonely or tired I am more vulnerable. So I try to fix the four detrimental conditions or be on high alert if I can't fix them. I also learned how triggers to an addictive behavior work, what specifically triggers me and then I try to avoid the triggers. And most importantly I got a sponsor who I am accountable to and who coaches me through testing moments. Before I thought it was impossible if I was in a room with an unguarded computer to not fall into porn so I relied on elaborate computer filters to safeguard myself but now I have found the best tool is self control because I could always get around internet filters and then I would kind of blame the filters for my fall. In society in general and also in many churches addictive tendencies are carefully hidden but sometimes we are only as sick as our secrets so in Celebrate Recovery we have a small group where we share our struggles as mostly believing men and it has helped me to see there are many other good Christian men and even pastors who struggle with the same thing I do. To be honest while I have compassion for the guys in the small group It also scares me from indulging more than I already have because some men I meet there are very hooked and cant seem to go a week without looking at porn and that scares me into doing my best to steer clear of it with my sponsors help and coaching.

Sometimes I wish we could have found tools like C.R. to help my previous marriage but a person can ultimately only go forward. Though hindsight is 20-20 none of us have the luxury of "do-overs" we have to turn the page, and move on to the next chapter, grab our second chance with both hands, and do our "do-overs" in the form of having learned from our mistakes in round one so we can do round two more intelligently.

After being hit on by younger women for years within my marriage I decided to find as attractive of girl as would want me.   Some felt I was crazy or even immoral for dating younger gals but I know the temptation I deal with as a successful Christian businessman and musician so I decided I would set the judgements of others aside and find a girl that would help me be a real good boy ! For me it had nothing to do with having a "trophy wife" or proving I could still get a younger woman but having walked a mile in my shoes I did what I thought was best for my life and set the bias of others aside.

So I dated younger women, got burned more than a couple times but eventually learned what qualities to look for and found an amazing good hearted girl from a good family and we have had an awesome marriage for over five years now ! Celebrating sex in marriage is God's plan !; free, fat free, enjoy as much as you want provision from an inventive, good heavenly Father !

Sometimes the devil makes a person think that the only good sex is in the club scene and the back seats in high school but that is a lie from Satan. The truth is not "the world has the good sex but the church has praise and worship." Sex done God's way in a long term bond with a loving partner is the best sex and surveys prove it.

Having this beautiful woman Mary has proved a great safe harbor for me. Even last night after finishing ministry in the Philippines a cute girl walked up behind me as I was walking back to my hotel and said, "hi, can I walk with you for a bit..." When I didn't respond she said, "I just want to walk with you to your hotel if you don't mind." I told her that I do mind because I am already taken. I had just had a lovely time with Mary whose beauty made that cute girl not even be a temptation for me! Praise God and kudos to the virgin Mary who came to rescue this sinner! I am doing my best to spare her from the mistakes I made in my first marriage. I look at it as God's grace to have given me a practice run and am trying to fail forward. Meanwhile Jaekyung and I have kept a respectful parenting relationship and I would even go so far as to say friendship.

You may just shake your head in scorn as I open up about the challenges I have faced but it is my hope that me opening up about my struggles, as well as my victories, may help you not feel isolated if you are a person dealing with a hurt, habit or hangup. A Christian witnessed to me once saying "its like I am up here on this plane with Jesus and all my problems are way beneath me!" When I became a Christian I realized, " HE LIED !" Gods word says "Be excellent at what is good, be innocent of evil " Thats great but I lost my innocence of evil since 3rd grade so what do I do now ? I renew my mind in God's word but I also told you some practical things I do that help me.

I wanted to include this ongoing struggle chapter in my testimony so that you don't think you are weird if you have come to Christ yet still have daily struggles with temptation. Celebrate Recovery is helpful because we step out of denial, blame, and excuses and just begin to deal with the hurts, habits and hangups we possess with the help of a supportive community. Doing recovery alone is almost impossible but forming relationships with others in recovery makes overcoming sin much more enjoyable and doable! We get by with a little help from our friends! If you have also failed in marriage it is also my hope that my story can help you overcome the condemnation that tries to set in and move forward and risk again!

When I was a worldly dude I looked at Christians as bored people who were missing out on life and particularly on sex. That misconception was perpetuated partly because the church never had anything to say about sex. My impression, as an outsider looking in, was that every real person knew sex was one of the most enjoyable things in life but that religious people thought it was dirty so they didn't talk about it but instead their pent up sexuality would come out sideways in expressions such as Catholic Fathers becoming pedophiles. So I think it is just best to discuss sexuality openly. Sex is mainstream and is headlining the thinking of half our race. Mary told me in some of the internet cafes in the Philippines 5 to 7 year olds are sitting there watching porn.

The joy of sex did not surprise God he was chairman of the committee that invented it; an idea came, "how about this going there" and God said "brilliant!" God created Adam and this knock out called Eve and he created sex. He put 4000 nerve endings in a mans penis and then took the design committee to staggering heights when he invented a clitoris with 8000 nerve endings and placed hundreds of pleasure sensors in the nipples and then hardwired all of them to simultaneously shoot off sparks in her genital sensory cortex !   He probably turned to the committee and said, "we just hit a home run boys now get to work!" Adam and Eve were naked in paradise and what do you think they did?! Then God looked down and said "It is good!" Not "It is evil and my people should not talk about it nor fully enjoy it!" He also provided an owners manual, the Bible, to govern it's use. Wherein he defined logical and loving limits so that the enjoyment of it, and the offspring created through it's enjoyment would be taken care of.

I have had casual sex out of marriage, before my conversion, and inside two marriages. The sex part was equally good in both but to be able to tell my beloved "I love you" and mean it both during and after sex to me makes God's provision in marriage superior. Maybe you can relate to my story and have not been truly fulfilled just having sex instead of making love. If so I hope my journey inspires you also. If you are a Christian and have downplayed God's amazing gift to your marriage scrub the barnacles off your boat and start enjoying !

People are like "Band-Aids" they only have so much glue. If you reuse a Band-Aid two or three times it doesn't stick very well.   God wanted people to save the gift of sex for marriage so that their allotment of glue would stick them neurologically to one person for life! Then within' that union experience unlimited unsurpassed pleasure! "But I am not married!" you lament! My heart goes out to you because I know how hard that is from recent experience. My advice would be to do your best to get married.

.I went through at least six failed relationships and $15,000.00 in trying before I found Mary. If at first you don't succeed try, try again!

Risk Again: Faith without action is useless the Bible says so we often need to put some effort into experiencing God's provision. People close to you may not have the nerve to talk straight to you but allow me to and don't hate me for it: get realistic; what kind of partner are you likely to attract? I wanted a cute younger partner so I devoted countless hours in the gym to sculpt my body to attract what I was fishing for. What type of mate you are realistically able to attract ? Now get busy and take action to find that person! Ask, seek, knock Gods word says. I have a friend who is about 200 pounds overweight and all her life has been believing God for a man who looks like a GQ Model. She feels like her prayers have gone unanswered but the reality is she either needed to be realistic about the type of guy she could attract or get to be the type of woman her target man would be looking for. There are many attitudes and other things that some need to adjust for a second chance so please don't think I dislike big people because this is the example I chose. Inner qualities are paramount but face it *"man looks on the outer appearance" 1 Samuel 16:7* In contrast to the friend I mentioned I had a big employee who decided she wanted to marry an athletic looking guy and instead of complaining got in the gym and lost 40 percent of her weight, looked amazing, found the man of her dreams, and is now happily married with kids. If you are content as a single and have the gift of being such forget everything I am saying, we will love you that way, but if you desire a mate take the needed action and find one. You gotta take some action if you want satisfaction !

Ch. 23 Funny Stuff That Happened

When I was about nine Dad loaded all us kids into his big wine colored Oldsmobile 98. Constructed like a tank with a 454 engine it was heavier than a full size GMC pickup and twice as durable. It was fun wheeling down to LA with Dad who was always in love with that area. We saw the Red Sea part at Universal Studios, visited the Le Brea Tar Pits, and took in a LA Rams game. After we had spent all our money we headed up the coast to San Francisco. By then we were on a tight budget and had started to eat the gallon cans of pork and beans Dad had dutifully packed in the trunk. We crossed the Golden Gate Bridge and started looking for a place to camp. When we couldn't find a campground we noticed a nice park on our left. We deduced that it must be a park so we took our chances and drove out onto it. The paved road was strangely narrow but we found the grass unequalled and set up our two tents. In the morning I unzipped the tent door and found some guys with golf clubs trying to get my attention and waving at me like I was a retard. I looked over and saw the flag. We had camped right on a golf green!!!

Don Hanks was always lots of fun. One day he got a new little four wheel drive jeep with no top on it. He drove up in the copper colored toy and said, "hey Bud you wanna go four wheelin?" Soon we were at the area we call the ski hill where they have motocross races. We were halfway up a really steep hill when Don says, "Oh no!" I look over and the steering wheel to his jeep has come off and it is in his hands! I thought that would be a good time to exit stage right so I bailed. (Since there was no top it was easy to jump out.) I thought pretty sure the jeep would slide sideways in the hill and roll, without a steering wheel, but Hondo kept his cool and managed to quickly slide the steering wheel back on enough for it to engage the grooved spline and work! Another time he and I and Roger Hale and Dave Finch took that rig hunting and the nastiest sleet storm came upon us! It was a wild ride home with us trying to hold a tarp over the jeep, which had no roof, clear back from Thompson River!

Don was a good mate and I enjoyed his happy go lucky demeanor. He was a hoot to party with but when we weren't partying we had good fun in the mountains camping. One time he and I were camping at the north side of Lion Lake. Don had brought his yellow 4 man raft and when we tucked in for the night he flipped it over and got on top of it which made a luxury camping bed. I meanwhile was next to him on the ground. Like a king he exulted about how extremely comfortable he was while the peon lay on the ground! I gave him a little smirk then pulled out my big sharp hunting knife and with a look of triumph stabbed his bed! The air came whooshing out and Donny sprung off his throne and should have rightly kicked my butt, and he could because he was a champion boxer, but he settled down and got a pretty good kick out of it himself! We laugh about it to this day!

When you are real stoned lots of stuff seems funny but here are a few things that actually were funny. (In a twisted un-sanctified sort of way.)

148

The Columbia Falls Wildcat football team had an away game in Libby Montana and Dan and I decided to party on down to Libby and raise some hell. The "Little Green Buger" had just come out of the shop for the engine rebuild and I remember it was one crazy hot little car that could break the tires loose with great ease. We passed people and flew on down to Libby and drank plenty of beer. Since we were out of town we thought it would be a good opportunity to enjoy some of the local cuisine and then dash away without paying. We went in some mom and pop kind of diner and ordered the most expensive stuff on the menu. After I finished the last breaded mushroom Dan said, "Ok time to go!" We got up purposefully and sauntered out the door without paying. As the door

closed behind us we broke into a sprint. The big waitress lady came bolting out the door and screamed, "you boys come back here or I'm calling the police!" When she said that we just stuck our chest out a little farther and peeled on down mainstreet to the getaway car and flew into the tan vinyl seats and screeched off out of town! We got a huge chuckle out of what the lady said to us and out of how we responded to her scary

threat! I am in no way advocating this practice. :) Dan was a really fun guy. He would make up these clever rhymes about politicians and teachers and was good at the quick put down.

Dan, Joe Purdy and I were going down the river in my Coleman canoe and drinking some beer. Joe could sing just like Elvis Presley so he stood up right in the middle of the canoe and started singing "Blue Suede Shoes." Joe was over 200 pounds and when he began gyrating those thighs the canoe plummeted dumping us all into the river. We all swam to shore ok but no one could save the canoe and it floated off leaving us up a creek without a paddle and without a canoe!

Dan and I grew up together and both loved dinosaurs and would play for hours with our plastic dinosaurs at age four and five. When I was about 8 my sister and I found this amazing horny toad that maybe some Arizona tourist had lost. We don't have them in Montana that I know of. It was super scaly and horned and colorful and looked just like a mini dinosaur. So Jamey and I told Dan, "we were rummaging through Dad's old books up in his attic and found a book about how to invent a Dinosaur! So we followed the recipe and created a real live dinosaur! When we showed Dan his eyes got so big and at first he thought for sure we had really done it!

 Another friend had a little too much fun with his girlfriend one night and they had a little one on the way. I urged him that they should get an abortion but he said no he really liked her and they decided to get married. (The odds against an 18 year old marrying a pregnant 16 year old and making it are not very good but they are still married now for over 30 years - he is a hard worker and she is cute and smart and it just worked.) Anyway my friend had me be one of his best men so I had this elaborate white tuxedo for the wedding. Meanwhile some girl asked me to be her escort because she was nominated for Homecoming queen. It was odd any girl would even ask me because I was a long haired crazy boy by then. I had this wild partying hat which was a Stetson that had belonged to my Grandpa Buckskin Jimmy and I had put a cool band on it and with a big Great Horned Owl feather stuck in the band. So to escort this girl I put on the elaborate tuxedo with the frilly shirt and topped it off with my beer stained Stetson. I must have been quite a sight! People thought it was pretty cool and I got a lot of compliments! After the game Scotty and I jumped in the little green buger and headed up the North Fork for a keggar. It was a fun night which got a little too fun when Roger gave me a hit and a half of acid. I was not as good of driver as my buddy Jay Winters, who I swear could have done stunts for "The Dukes of Hazard," but I was pretty tight even when I was plowed. As Scotty and I left the keggar Snortin' George asked for a ride. (He was an up the line crazy guy who had just come back from the army. He had a reputation as an absolutely crazy driver.) As the acid kicked in my lead foot became totally unhinged. I remember going into a controlled slide on a gravel road and passing one or two cars in the midst of the controlled slide. I was having great fun and Scotty was laughing so loud. We noticed George was really quiet in the back seat. But when I passed the last car George's white knuckles grabbed the back of our headrests and he billowed, "stop the car I'm gettin' out." I kindly assured him I would cool my jets and let him out at the Blue Moon but if my memory serves me correctly I think he just got out there! Scott and I found that pretty hilarious since he was known to be such a wild driver himself. Scott would tell that story at many a party!

We enjoyed going to "The Midway Drive In" by "The Blue Moon Saloon". The drive in is gone now but the iconic Blue Moon seems forever the same. The owner does all his own bouncing and I don't think anyone will be able to evict him from his location! The Drive-In had a per car price rather than a per person price. Maybe that is why they went out of business because us kids could fit at least 4 extra heads in the trunk! This was one of the funnest places to just walk around and create mischief. One time me and the boys were cruising the lot on our Chevrolegs and we noticed a car kind of moving up and down. Upon further inspection we found the back-up catcher for my baseball team in the back seat with his gal. Us four guys grabbed the back bumper and started bouncing the car up and down vigorously. The girl was an underclassmen I once had the hots for. She got so mad she came storming out of the back door in only her bra and undies reading us guys the riot act! The guy was trying to back her up the best he could but his face was rather blushed!

Another time at the drive-in my best friend Jay brought these 2 girls to our car. He and Theresa got in the back seat and started to make out. That left me up front with Joan. Joan was a nice girl and a friend of my older sister Jamey. An upper classmen that wasn't really my type. But I was trying to be hospitable so I started putting a few little moves on her like putting my hand on her leg. In our heart we both knew the chemistry wasn't there and she was so much older so when I did she just looked at me and said with a smile…"Buddy… I don't think so." To me it was awkward enough to be included here in my funny stuff epilogue.

Another funny story along these lines was when I took our class' track star Kiris to the Park Theatre. All the up-perclassmen cheerleaders were sitting behind us with Kelly Blades and Sherri Hart. When I put my arm around Kiris for the first time ever my arm snagged some ABC gum wad and it ended up in Kiris' fine hair! It was so em-barrassing to have the upperclass cheerleaders help her pick gum out of her hair the rest of the night !

152

Looking back on these times I know some of them were illegal and others were dangerous but there is something to be said for friends having fun together. Not all but it seems many Christians get so serious that they kind of forget to have fun. Pastor Randy Phillips last week said that he came from a fundamentalist Christian home. He said that his home took the fun out of the word though and all that was left was "mentalist." There are some serious aspects of the Christian faith but I want to figure out how to hold on to the truths of the faith without becoming a mentalist! I don't think God is even all that serious until sin messed things up and he had to fix it at a very high cost. I think God is a good time sort of being at heart.

Not that drinking too much is a good idea but I think when you are real drunk you can survive a pretty brisk collision sometimes because your body is so loose. Once Jay and I were driving my 400 Polaris Snowmobile at absolute top speed (55 m.p.h) and the left ski came detached from the rod and plunged straight down into the snow on the gravel part of the lower dam road. When it did it caused the whole snowcat to begin to roll end over end. It threw us off then did at least a couple end over end rolls!!! The snowmobile was strewn all over the road and we literally picked it up in a box but we were fine and thought it was funny!!

I gave Dan, Todd, and Sam a pretty good jolt one night when without warning I just leaped off the bridge in Whitefish which goes over the train tracks. The bridge is about 25 feet off the ground but I casually spied a train box car full of wheat. I thought it would provide a soft landing and the top of the car was only about 15 feet below me so I just said to my friends, "we'll see you guys later!," Amidst their gasps of surprise I just leaped over the side rails !

Once in the air I thought to myself, "Oh no what if I plunge like 3 feet into the wheat and suffocate." Fortunately when I hit the wheat it did provide some cushion but I didn't sink into it much. When I climbed down and rejoined them they thought it was pretty cool and crazy! Maybe it was just too bad we didn't have phones to video stuff back then !

Part of that craziness came from the fact that I was a good athlete but when I turned stoner as a freshman I no longer played baseball, football or basketball. Instead I channelled my athleticism into stuff like hookybobbing. This is when you run up behind a car, van, or truck, without them seeing you, and grab hold of the bumper then go sliding along on the icy street. Its a blast unless you hit a spot of bare pavement then the fun ends in a hurty! I invented another way to do it which was to open the passenger side door when I was riding shotgun then put my right hand on the door and put my left hand on the seat and my right hand on the door pull and whiz along the ice half way out of a pick up! It was another good way to build my reputation as a wild and crazy guy! Dan and I always wanted to be stunt men and one time we actually got to be in a movie that shot in the Flathead Valley called "Winterhawk." It was about an Indian. We rolled down the hillside like people being shot although they didn't include that part in the movie but we were actually in the movie!

Dad in his day was a real community leader and started dances in the back of the Honeyberry Farm so kids could have something to do that didn't involve alcohol. My older sisters Sharlon and Bonni were in that sensitive age; 15 and 17 and Bonni was a respected cheerleader and popular girl. Right in the middle of the dance with a packed house from their High School the lights go down and the curtains open and there is Dad in a long black Indian wig and says, "all right kids now we are going to all learn to Indian Dance ! He proceeds to circle in dance and do all his "hi yi yi yi's" as most of the audience heads to their car for a beer shaking their heads in disbelief. Bonni was horrified that her Dad embarrassed her so completely but to make matters worse back at school on Monday when teacher Doug Follet was doing the roll call when he got to Bonni's name he calls out "Minihaha!" Dad once locked Jamey and I in a room and tried to get us to memorize "Hiawatha" the poem. He would almost cry when he read it ! :)

Dad was a community leader and Boy Scout headmaster

One last fun story. Dad was always fascinated with some trumpet player named Al. So he bought me a trumpet. I kinda liked making noise with the thing and practiced some till everyone in my household insisted I only practice far away in the forest. But Jamey and I loved to make prank phone calls so she and I developed suave TV host type voices then one of us would call up someone and say, "This is KGEZ radio and you have been randomly selected to win $500.00 if you can name this tune! Are you willing to participate in our live show and try to name the following tune?" Many would reply with enthusiasm "Yeah go ahead and play it!" Then Jamey would put the speaking end of the old style telephone right at the end of my trumpet and I would give an elephantine blast! They probably didn't think it was very funny but kids in a town of 500 have to find some way to get their kicks !

Chapter 24 The Best Drug I Ever Found

I tried numerous drugs including all grades of pot ranging from shit weed from the ditches of Mexico which we would buy for $40.00 an ounce to Sensimillion that was over $200.00 an ounce. My favorite was sweet gummy Hawaiian Afghani hashish, Quaaludes, Valium, Percodans, Codeine, Morphine, LSD, Peyote Cactus, Mushrooms and household items that sizzle your brain cells. I stopped short of Heroine when an older guy offered me the needle at a party. And I am glad they didn't have Meth or Crack when I was a user although I snorted plenty of Coke and made Cocaine joints called Cocoa Puffs. (I never liked Coke because I am hyper already.)

I cannot deny that some of these allowed me to travel the universe in style but the greatest high I ever experienced came when I came to know Jesus the Anointed One personally. (Christ means Anointed One…He is anointed to break the yoke of whatever binds you.) The greatest drug I ever found was the Holy Spirit. When I first came to Jesus this power would come upon my mind and inner person. It felt like the purest Sensimilia without any blurry side effects. It felt like an inner power that could make me run faster, think smarter, and have confidence where before I had fear. The coolest thing of all is that when I got done trippin' on the Holy Spirit there were no negative side effects but plenty of good side effects such as wisdom, peace and closeness to God. It was the only trip I found that brought me up without then taking me even further down. Wow, if I could just figure out a way to bottle and sell this stuff I would sure make more money than when I used to sell pot! But the really good news is that it is free! The best drug in the world is free! No wonder they call the gospel

GOOD NEWS! In the early days of my salvation this power would just hit me without me even asking for it. One time I was in the library of Columbia Falls High and the presence of God came on me so strong I had to put my hand on the library table to steady myself so I wouldn't fall over. Other times I would be telling people about what Jesus had done in my life and that power would be on me so strong that I was as bold as a Lion. Many people could see that power in my face and in my eyes. The first time my parole officer saw me, after my soul was filled with God's Spirit, he took one look at me and said something like, "Buddy you are not even the same person, I don't know what it is about you now but your entire countenance has changed." I told him, "God changed my life!"

It was a clean, clear rush that was similar to a high grade pot but when the high subsidedI felt energized and focused not spaced out and lethargic. This same feeling often comes on me when I lead worship or preach God's word. That is partly why I love doing that is because of the feeling I get when the Holy Spirit   Most the time as a believer I do not feel the Holy Spirit much in my daily experience but at least my mind is clear.

I have known plenty of Christians who have said that its OK to keep smokin' a little weed. But the Holy Spirit is jealous and will back off from you when you put a different spirit into your spirit. The Greek word pharmacea is where we get our word Pharmaceutical from and the word means sorcery. I believe pot and other drugs are like sorcery in that it alters your state of mind. But if you will plug into Jesus Christ and His church you will get high on the Most High and experience the best high that you could ever imagine. The only problem is that it can take more effort to do that. With refer you just buy some, put a "Bic" to it and inhale. With God's high I found out that as a new baby Christian he doused me real good without much effort but now that I am more mature it seems I need to read his word, get my lazy bottom to church on time, sing worship songs, and put some effort into it sometimes before the real good high returns. That is why Jesus said the way is narrow that leads to life and few there be that find it because most people give in to their flesh and just light up.

I have many friends who still use pot and if they want to waste their money on a low grade high when they could be enjoying the free high I am on that is their business but if you are contemplating the switch know that God will never take anything away from you without giving you something even better in return.   "Be not drunk with wine wherein is excess but instead be filled with the Spirit speaking to one another in psalms, hymns, and spiritual songs." Ephesians   I don't think the Bible is against a half a glass of wine with dinner or a beer with your fries if it is not a trigger for you to get drunk but if you have been depending on drugs and alcohol to get you high I would like to recommend that you get high on the Most High! You will never want to go back to substances that destroy your brain cells, memory, lungs, or liver to get high again!

People say there are many roads to God and some people like me before coming to Christ even believed the collective beauty of creation -- the mountains, sky, tall trees and sun -- were in and of themselves God. But I never felt the greatest drug of all in any other road to God other than God the Father confirming that His Son Jesus Christ is the one and only way to really get to God!

158

God! There might be other roads toward God but there is only one road that actually gets you there! And when you take that road God the Father pours into the deep dry place of your soul the precious Holy Spirit.

I'm talkin' bout a feelin' a feelin' that I get
when I get into the Spirit and really get met,
It's a feelin' kinda holy, a feeling' kinda high,
feelin' that flows from the River of Life.

There's a feelin' that you get when you do good at a sport, and a feelin' that you get when you take some coke to snort. There's a feelin' that you get when you kiss a girl, but this Holy Ghost feelin' is outa this world!

Theres a feelin' that you get when you make alotta money and a feelin' that you get when you're jokin' and funny. There's a feelin' that you get when you pass a test! But this Holy Ghost Feelin' is better than the best!

Every summer in Hungry Horse Bible camp there is a RAIN camp with Jim and Ramona Rickard. There were a couple times being prayed for by them that I just got blasted by the Holy Ghost where almost a drug like wow coursed through my whole being! But no negative side effects!

Check out R.A.I.N. Ministries International and "Revival in The Rockies" at Glacier Bible Camp in Hungry Horse ! This ministry will change your life and help you experience the risen Christ through his Holy Spirit and signs and wonders.

Ch. 25 How did an Avid Evolutionist Believe in the Bible?

I had experienced an undeniable encounter with the living Christ but my head was still filled with years of indoctrination in Evolution. So especially in the first few weeks after my conversion nagging doubts would bombard my mind that all these incidents of apparent divine intervention were just coincidences and that Jesus was not really alive today. I would tell myself, "You have seen enough miracles do not doubt in the dark what you saw in the light!" As an atheist son of an atheist and as a former debater of evolution I had some huge intellectual concerns with the Bible. I took these concerns to God in prayer, "God I am having a terrible time believing in the literal return of Christ on the clouds, in Noah's ark, in Jonah and the whale, and in creation. Would you please help me."

I found through research that there are very few "missing links" but that each kind of species appeared intact and developed in the fossil record...Inarguably evolution has taken place within each species through breeding but, after studying Dr. Duane Gish, I concluded that the fossil record did not support evolution as the "origin of the species." Instead men who wanted to live proud or promiscuous lives came up with the theory to excuse themselves from giving an account to creator God. This thought was confirmed to me as I sat by the river and read Romans 1:20-27 "God's creativity, power, and love are clearly portrayed in his creation. But even though men beheld God in creation they thanklessly rejected him. Professing themselves to be wise they became fools and exchanged the truth of God for a lie and their foolish hearts were darkened. So God said, "Ok you want me to leave your life then I will." And when He did, utter darkness enfolded them insomuch that they even exchanged natural relations for homosexual relations."

I had experienced a life changing encounter with the risen Jesus Christ! I could not remain sane and deny the way he was pursuing my life yet the book my new faith was based on, the Bible. Seemed to contain outlandish stories my intellect could not swallow such as Jonah being swallowed by the whale. So I researched the incident and found that firstly the Hebrew word is not whale it is " great fish."

Nick Squires reported that a man was swallowed by a Great White Shark in Sydney Australia but survived the incident and lived to tell about it. This happened at 12:01AM GMT 24 Jan. 2007.

Also a man was swallowed by a whale at an aquarium in Chicago;

Chicago, IL – An Arkansas man is alive after being swallowed by a whale on Saturday while visiting the Shedd Aquarium. Jonah Anderson, 24, is being treated for mild dehydration at Chicago's Mercy Medical Center after being regurgitated early this morning.

The incident happened while viewing the Beluga Whale exhibit at Shedd. Witnesses say the whale, Puiji, came out of the pool, grabbed Anderson, and proceeded to swallow him whole...

http://www.rockcitytimes.com/local-m...hedd-aquarium/

I did not find conclusive proof that a man has lived after being swallowed by a large fish but there are several true incidents of similar events so I felt the Jonah story was not enough to dissuade me from my new faith. I had an experience in which I felt like a modern day Jonah. I met my first wife Jaekyung in Kenya and Uganda and we both desired to return to Uganda to do mission work. After our marriage we began making concrete plans to return to Uganda. During that summer the Spirit of God visited me one night and spoke "Jamaica" to me. God has led me through the inner witness of the Holy Spirit and the word of God many times but on several occasions God has spoken to me not audibly but very very clearly in my Spirit. I prayed for Jamaica after this but kept making plans for Africa. But nothing was lining up or working out for Africa so I declared a 3 day fast to seek God for direction. On the second day of the fast my nieces and nephews were visiting and Halladay Quist asked, "Uncle James can we come with you to Africa and see the elephants and lions?" I smiled and replied something about how nice it would be to take them. I had not told anybody that God had spoken Jamaica so strong to me recently. Then my nephew Harley Hanks who was about 5 got up with fire in his eye, pointed his finger at me and exclaimed, "But James, what about JAMAICA?!!! Are you going to Jamaica?!! Are you ?!" He was so fiery that I felt like running away from him so I escaped into my bathroom. In the bathroom I kept a Bible and when I opened it my eyes fell on the scripture, "And the Lord spoke to Jonah a second time saying…" I knew that the oracle through Harley was God's second command for me to go to Jamaica. We went, led hundreds of people to Christ, started a small church, I had a newspaper column in Montego Bay's largest newspaper, and Josiah our son was born there. It was a word of the Lord similar to what Jonah had received so I figure if God can deal with

162

a guy that convincingly I should not allow the account of Jonah and the whale to dissuade my faith.

As I researched Noah's Ark I found that no other ancient story appears as often in isolated cultures who had no way of collaborating their stories. Over 500 ubiquitous flood stories exist from every culture in every corner of the globe from the present dating back to the dawn of writing.

I found another convincing factoid in Josh McDowell's "Evidence That Demands a Verdict" "John Whitcomb and Henry Morris, in their book "The Genesis Flood" analyzed the pertinent data regarding the carrying capacity of the ark; they note that the ark would have been 437.5 feet in length, 72.92 feet in width, and 43.75 feet in height. (figuring from 17.5 inches per cubit). The ark had three decks (Genesis 6:16). So the carrying capacity of the ark would, therefore be equal to 522 standard railroad stock cars each of which could carry 240 sheep." They went on to determine that a couple from each main species in the earths 17,600 primary species could have been housed and fed in a vessel of said magnitude.

This information about Noah's Ark helped my intellect see it as a plausible option then I came into my living room just a week or two after my conversion and there on the tube was a vivid portrayal of dirty hecklers shaking their fists at Noah... they reminded me of the people in my world who were now shaking their fists at me. And then the rains came and they began to scream as the ark began to rise. Somehow God used that simple T.V. show to help me believe.

I slowly evolved from atheism to believing that God was a mystical collection of all living energy. Kind of like the Star Wars concept of the universal force. So to now conceptualize God as a person named Jesus who would come again in the clouds in the shape of a man was just way too far fetched even for my converted mind to believe. I asked God to help me swallow that pill. God saw fit to forever erase my doubts by allowing me to experience it all in a vision of the night that was more real than real life. Here is how it happened; one night in my dream the world had become very dark and I was suffering greatly for my bold faith. I was in almost some form of exile and as I looked out over a lake I inwardly groaned, "how long O Lord must I suffer this persecution?" A shimmer on the lake I was watching turned into a twinkle then the lake and the mountains behind the lake began getting more and more beautiful until the modest landscape became as stunning as the majestic panorama of Glacier Park's mountains on a perfect day. The mountains were white and were glowing as if illuminated from within. Then the beauty of the mountains became intensified beyond any beauty I had ever seen on this earth and then I knew I was looking at heavenly mountains! As the lake and mountains grew in heavenly splendor they also grew whiter till they were shining white. At the same time it was as if someone extinguished the sun and the moon and totally turned off all the lights in the whole universe. The sky became utterly black (But the mountains and lake were still luminescent.) Then a monumental thunderclap cracked open the pitch black sky from East to West. Out of the narrow crack came heavenly furls of shining white cloudy mist. It was a mist that seemed to contain the presence of God. Then I was caught up by an invisible elevator and began to rise up into the sky! I rose up higher and higher then even in the dream I could feel the tangible presence of God very strong and then the wonderful sensation intensified. At that moment through the mist I could see this huge white being on an enormous white throne. The gigantic being and the throne were shining with a dazzling light that was both peaceful and powerful but didn't hurt my eyes. I knew it was the Lord in all His beauty but he was somewhat obscured by the mist. Then the veil of misty cloud filtered away from the throne and I saw the glorified Jesus face to face! His eyes were glowing like a fire and the rest of him was ultra white. I felt such incredible love but at the same time I felt really dirty in his super-clean presence. But even though I felt dirty I experienced absolutely perfect peace and love. I soaked it in and I wanted to bask forever in the perfect peace and love that was radiating through my whole body..... then bam I woke up! This dream was even more real than real life and it was like my body was really there so I was so ticked off when I woke up because it was the greatest sensation my body had ever experienced and I could still feel that amazing holy peace and flawless love as a physical sensation in my body. Even though I was awake now the presence was still on me so strong that I felt like that giant Q-tip that the doctor pulls out of the Nitrous Oxide tank before freezing off a wart. I was sizzling and crackling with heaven's power. In those early days several people commented to me that I was glowing with the Holy Spirit's power. For the longest time I only told 3 or 4 of my closest friends about this encounter. It seemed too holy to even speak of. Yet as I am becoming older now I desired to put it in this book in order for the power of it to endure to the next generation.

The effect of this vision seemed to propel me around the world. I was "on fire" with the gospel message. It burned in my belly as I told friends and family in the Flathead Valley. Ultimately it became a source of inward propulsion that empowered me to declare Christ in many nations of the world before crowds as large as 2 or 3,000 people and thrice on TV. Satan has hit me with blow after severe blow of the best he can devise but the flame is still lit even though the repeated assaults have at times dampened the heat of the fire. Even through severe hardship such as my Christian wife leaving me, and my daughter not talking to me for over a year, and losing all four of my houses in the divorce so I had to sleep in my pickup I have never quit loving the Lord or quit going to church every Sunday and reading my Bible every day. This practice has been like a rudder enabling my spiritual ship to stay on course even through intense storms or somewhat self induced difficulties. I did quit preaching for awhile to try to get my family back together but I eventually realized my X and my kids were gonna do what they were gonna do but I must do what I need to do and that is to love and serve the Lord. So I began preaching again and now seem to have an even larger ministry than before the divorce in that I help minister to and guide 16 churches in India and 14 churches in the Philippines as well as preach regularly to a church in Austin, Texas.

In the circles I frequented B.C. it was ok to talk about God, or even Jesus, as a great teacher, but to talk about the Bible as a credible book was really taboo. Yet as God revealed Himself to me more and more through the radical transformation of my life, through the vision I just described, through educating my intellect concerning the shortfalls of the evolution theory, and through seeing good Christian love lived out before me in the church I attended by people like Todd and Marlene Hansen, Sally and Dennis Emerson, Tom Brake, Don and Jim Downing and John Attard. Finally I told myself, "you have seen enough radical proof that Jesus is alive like the Bible says he is, Evolution takes great faith to believe now it is time to just take the step of faith to believe the Bible is God's word and settle that in your mind." So one evening, about a month after my conversion, I just decided to believe that the Bible is God's word. That night I had the most demonic dream: Now my mother Laverne Olga Willows had become a believer about 7 years before she died. She suffered a debilitating aneurism stroke which paralyzed the right side of her brain and the left side of her body. She became desperate for God one night, after the stroke, and pleaded to my sister Bonni to help her find faith one night. Bonni called a priest who said she was out of his district then she began to pray on her own. She told me she felt very horrible accusing thoughts invade her mind but then she called a Christian friend and kept praying till she felt the presence of Jesus wash her mind, soul, and body. With eyes aglow she told Mom, "Mom, I have found God!" She led Mom to Christ then Mom became active in "The Hungry Horse Chapel"

(Pic: George Moore: Pastor who had dream about me being saved & Todd Hansen) and even partially donated the land that their new sanctuary is built on. She quietly lived out her faith as well as she could in her paralyzed state. I am sure she prayed much for me. Now my Grandma Zerbin was a very strong Christian and had accurate visions and dreams at times. One night mom went into a coma and died. I was so crazy at the time that I went partying that night and drove through the ditch to pass people and ended up at a Keggar that got busted and I ended up at the jail till 3 AM.

But the next morning the phone rang and it was Grandma. I answered and Grandma said, "Laverne is dead isn't she?, I said "yes Grandma how did you possibly know?" She replied, "last night I had a dream and saw her in a beautiful blue dress walking briskly through the mountains without her crutches and I knew for sure the Lord had taken her home to Heaven." I said, "wow Grandma that is pretty amazing because she did die yesterday afternoon!" But getting back to my demonic dream the night I decided to believe the Bible; in the very realistic dream my mother appeared to me and she was still paralyzed and looked very sick, she told me, "don't believe in Jesus and the Bible Buddy, it is all a LIE! SEE! I am still paralyzed." At that exact moment I was wakened by an ear piercing screech "YOOOWWWLLLL!" I felt the presence of Satan in the room so strong that I could not physically move. I was actually paralyzed by a demon and a horrible fear coursed through my mind. We did not have cats but I saw through the corner of my eye a black cat that had somehow snuck in and it let out another deafening Halloween "YOOOWWWLLL!"! I finally fought against that paralyzed feeling enough to turn the light on and open my Bible to read a reassuring Psalm. I knew my declaration of faith in God's word had prompted Satan to attack me that night. Because the word of God is a living book unlike any other which has the power to replace darkness with light, sickness with health, poverty with prosperity, and fear with faith. Satan did not want to lose me. Because in that very bed I had stripped foxy Sam and had so much fun, in that very bed my best friend wakened me on the previous New Years Eve with his wiener out pissing all over the room! (He was so drunk) In that very bed I had smoked pot with my friends and lusted over "Penthouse" magazines. It made Satan angry that now I was reading my Bible and declaring my faith in God's word. But that night the lying Devil kind of shot himself in the foot because the attack was so blatant that it actually served to strengthen my faith. It seemed the harder I pressed in to God, the harder Satan fought me. I had listened to Black Sabbath lyrics which sang, "My name is Lucifer please take my hand." I had not even believed he was real at the time but once the Christ and mighty prayers of God's people set me free the enemy's activity became very blatant also.

*Just a quick story; When I was Pastor of Love and Faith Church a woman named who had a home for needy girls called and said, "Pastor one of our girls has had guttural voices all night long and even bite marks on her arms." I replied, "bring her down to the church, we will minister to her." At first we tried to just lovingly counsel her to no avail, it was like talking to a brick. Then Jaekyung said, "you wicked spirit come out of her in Jesus name!" At that she bolted for the door and I was led of the Lord to block the door and hold her from thrashing. (I would normally never block a door as people have free will but in this case her free will had been over ridden by Satan.) She continued to thrash about as Jaekyung applied the anointing oil. I was holding her and praying. During the next half hour or so we cast the evil spirit out and she sat so peacefully receiving our words of love and instruction. We received a report in the coming weeks of great blessing and spiritual growth in the young lady.

When a church walks in that level of authority it becomes quite a target for the enemy and he cooked up a scheme to take us out but we pick up the pieces and keep running the race set before us. Warriors once wounded who then recover have a quality that in war is called "The Eye of the Tiger". I may have some scars but I still have some fire and am now involved in 30 churches!

I can't recall exactly who was on the corner with us during my "night to remember."   I know it was Scott Downing, Mark Schaefer, Alan Birky, Roger Walters, and ??? I also know Jim Downing watched me have the gun pointed at my head and saw me get beat up. On May 4, 2015 however I ran into my old friend Danny Seliger. Dan was a good boxer and wrestler who came to Christ at about the same time I did. On May 4 we began to muse about old times and he started talking about my fateful night.
 "Wow Danny you were there too!? I exclaimed! He affirmed that he was there on the corner too that night so I asked him what he remembered: (It fit too because I knew there were 5 or 6 of us I just couldn't recall exactly who all of them were.)

Danny;
We were all hanging around on the corner and after the guys in the big black truck got mad one started waving a gun around and told us to get off that corner. We asked them which corner they wanted us to go to and they just cussed. As we were all dispersing either Mark Schaefer or Buddy leaped over the front end of the truck and it looked like they hardly even touched the hood! I couldn't believe my eyes!

Buddy; "What do you remember happening after that? Did you see me and their leader locking horns?"
Danny; "No we all ran away!"   Buddy: "Thanks a lot pal! lol"

Ch 27 Seedbed of My Crazed Life: The Home

Most of the craziness I went through could have been prevented by a normal home life. My Dad was a winsome go-getter who owned most of the town and my mother was a smart ambitious woman also. In their day they were community leaders and model citizens but their marriage was like many in that it had been driven far too hard with too many oil changes skipped and by the time I came around sparks were flying constantly. Mom and Dad stayed together till I was six. I really liked being at the table together with them and having them ask me how school (first grade) went. But they had horrible terrifying fights. Jamey and I built a fort in the basement out of couch cushions to try to insulate ourselves from the high decibel combat and to hide from them. (We thought the combat might turn upon us next.) One night the screaming was so intense that we were especially terrified. Then we heard Dad discover Mom's "medicinal" brandy. Next thing we heard was a bottle shatter and a piercing scream. Finally, during a brief lull in the screaming, Dad called me up into his bedroom and told me he was moving to his business. He said he hoped that I would come live with him as much as possible - he was a fun Dad when he wasn't mad - so I kind of wanted to but I really felt torn by it all.

 At that time divorce was a shameful thing so they never got divorced but just lived separate. This wasn't too bad until Mom had a stroke when I was nine. The aneurism took half her mind and half her body. It left her as an invalid who could barely get around with the help of a crutch. Certain functions of her brain no longer worked. So instead of having a parent in the home we almost needed to parent her. I remember many nights when Jamey or I would need to go empty her bed pan and sometimes Jamey had to clean her bottom. Dad came home every other day to bathe her, bring groceries, and scream at us kids but that was about the extent of his involvement. I sincerely admire the fact that he didn't get another girlfriend till we graduated from high school and that he just didn't leave completely! Not many guys today would support an invalid wife for 7 years but Dad did his best. Our home had 0 spiritual guidance and almost no parental guidance. It was full of darkness and nightmares with us kids doing crazy stuff like playing strip poker with our friends, playing Ouji board, and staying out till 3 A.M. partying even as 7th graders. Many Friday and Saturday nights I would come home drunk and go puke in the bathroom as Mom tried to share her concern but I would just cuss at her. At times I would bring girls home to sleep with me and Mom tried to curtail this but just couldn't since she was paralyzed. (And since Dad had a huge stack of "Playboys" and believed so strongly in evolution/survival of the fittest he wouldn't curtail that activity even if he knew.)   Mom cared very much for me since I was the only son.

 The one good thing that happened to Mom through the paralysis is that she came to know Jesus in a personal way and started going to a Spirit Filled church.   She didn't really preach to us but really tried to be the best example she could given her circumstances. One time she had a serious tailspin and grew much worse. We were sure her days were numbered but then people from the church kept coming over and going in her room behind closed doors. After a few days of this she walked out of her room with only her small cane and was so greatly improved! At the time I had no idea what was going on but now I know they were praying and it was working! The Christians were coming into our demon infested home and breaking the power and ministering healing to her. But some time later she looked at me with a crazed look and gave a low shocked bawl then went into a coma. A few days later she died. The next morning our Christian Grandma phoned up and asked, "Laverne is gone isn't she?" I replied, "yes Grandma, how did you know?" She replied, "last night I had a dream that she was in a beautiful blue dress and she was leaping happily in the beautiful mountains without her crutch - so I knew she had gone home to be with the Lord!" I thought it was pretty amazing that Grandma knew of Mom's death but I was so hardened that that very night I dropped some acid and did more of my crazy driving antics. Back then Hwy. 93 S. was a two lane. There was oncoming traffic so I took to the shoulder and passed several cars through the gravel to the right of the pavement. I narrowly missed reflectors but I was good at what I did and controlled the Green Buger as I re-entered the pavement at 70 m.p.h. in front of the string of cars who couldn't quite believe what had happened. Later that night a group of cops busted a keggar I was at in the forest. Being fast I sprinted off into the woods with nary a policeman trailing me but they refused to leave the grounds. I got tired of shivering in the forest so I came out after a long while before my "Little Green Buger" was impounded. I ended up the night detained at the cop shop where I was ticketed but didn't have to go to spend the night in jail.

The family is so key to the overall health of kids, but many homes do not have the power or light of Christ to help keep the darkness out. Many marriages start out hopeful but get too busy and forget to refuel. My home had once been a wonderful place with Dad telling us

Tarzan stories and Mom lovingly tucking us in at night but then it was broken and became a place of screaming and nightmares. Supervision ceased. Then I became wild.

Relationships are like check books in that we can only deal with expenses to the degree we make deposits into our accounts. If we have more outgoing cash than incoming deposits they bounce. I bounced a major relationship but I am not the first Christian man to do so and I probably won't be the last. I've learned from the pain.

Ch. 28 LIFE TODAY

When I got wonderfully saved and converted I determined to serve Christ for the rest of my life period. Relationship with him has been a very uplifting aspect of my life even through difficult times. On the other hand I think anyone who determines to never miss church and read God's word every day and do their utmost to work for Christ will receive minor and major attacks of our enemy Satan; In speaking of our adversary Bob Dylan penned the line, "using every angle till the battle's lost or won! Yet even though Christian leaders have screwed me over at times and those I trusted the most have turned away when I needed them the most God has never left me or forsaken me! He has helped me keep moving forward even in ministry through trials such as the divorce. Since the divorce I have conducted regular ministry in the Philippines insomuch that we now have 13 churches I minister to regularly and I did many joyful concert crusades in India and we now have 16 churches I work with regularly there! God continues to provide a few reliable friends and he continues to open doors for ministry. Just yesterday I preached under a strong anointing to a growing congregation in Round Rock, Texas and then last night the local radio station in Austin invited me to come minister to their audience in a three hour interview! They also said they would add many of the songs on my CD to their playlist.!   KNLE 88.1 FM in Austin plays my music regularly and you can see many of my music videos on **YouTube** such as "Through Faiths Eyes - *James Willows* - and "Runnin' on Love" or "Jesus in my Light; which is this story in song."

Mary and I in our winter home Austin, Texas 2018

Paul the apostle went through joyful times in his life and also heart ache in relationships and ministry but year after year he just kept pressing for the mark of the high calling of God in Christ Jesus! Then finally one day he said "I have fought the good fight, I have finished the race, I have kept the faith!" 1 Tim. 4:7 That's my goal !

I am believing God that even the great setback I have experienced in this divorce will be a setup for a greater comeback just like it was for Job in the end. God guided me after a fast to an amazing wife Mary Jane Torion Willows and we get along very well and serve God together for 3 years now!   I also thank God that I have a good parenting relationship with Jaekyung and this Sunday will watch my son Abe graduate at the Wharton School of Business, Huck Land has grown each year and is becoming famous! Glory to God for keeping me showing up every day without missing for 27 years ! I never missed a game in baseball so I never miss work now !

Chapter 29   To The Nations!

The third verse of my testimony song says "I felt like telling the world 'bout what He did.   God said "That's my plan, go do it kid " Africa, China and Jamaica too I tell 'em what he did for me, he can do for you!

I have a burning desire to reach the people of the world with this life changing story and the good news of the freedom that is available in Jesus Christ!

1981 I began a Youth With A Mission DTS training program then did a three month outreach with YWAM in the island of Kauai, Hawaii.

1982 Street Ministry at Spring Break Fort Lauderdale

1983 Did University of the Nations' 9 month School of Biblical Studies then conducted 4 months of street ministry in Seattle, San Francisco, L.A. during the '84 Olympics. Then deep into Mexico where I gave a concert for the city of Zijuatenejo and led dozens to Christ.

1985   A year of school and evangelism with Abbot Loop Christian Fellowship in Anchorage Alaska.

1986   6 months of doing crusades and speaking in schools in Uganda and Kenya East Africa with YWAM

1987 7 months of being on staff at YWAM in Nuneaton, England. Lecturing and taking students for evangelism

1989-90 Full time missionaries in Jamaica where we planted a church.

1991 3 months conducting a Bible School in Russia with 200 students three times a week through "Storehouse Ministries International." Ed & Shirley Allen !

1991 - 2001 Conducting large Crusades in many Nations as an Evangelist sent out of New Covenant Fellowship of Columbia Falls, Montana.

Since that time I planted two more churches, Valley Victory Church in Kalispell, MT. and Love and Faith Fellowship in Kalispell, MT. Both served hundreds of people and ministered in the community over a decade each.

I have done major crusades in The Ivory Coast, Kenya, Uganda, South Africa, Botswana, The Philippines, India, Mexico, Jamaica, Russia and have ministered to some extent in 24 other countries.

My ministry today focuses on planting and strengthening a network of 14 Churches in Mindanao Island, Philippines and 16 Churches in Southern India. As well as ministry in a music ministry based in Austin Texas.

At The Freedom Crusade in Kapalong, Philippines we sang and I preached to about 2,000 people per night with about 200 responding to the nightly call for salvation

In the Freedom Crusades local churches sponsor the event then I put together a band to draw people and the local Pastors care for converts.

Here I am preaching in Kapalong with my good friend Bishop Edgar V. Labus who oversees the 14 churches we worked together to plant and establish in the Philippines.

Ministering Music in Chennai, India where I came close to being stoned by 125 militant Hindus

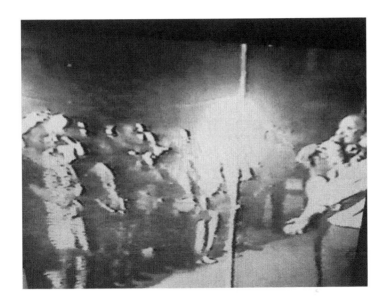

Above :   At the altar call of my largest crusade in Abidjan, Ivory Coast where I preached to about 3,000 people most of whom were unbelievers. Many of the cities largest, strongest men came to Christ that night.

On TV in Russia after giving a concert at an academy for Models ! Yay God ! That was OK !

With my friend Pastor Leonard Kanyama in Johannesburg, South Africa and also Botswana.

Just last night I

preached on a radio station here in Austin TX where they play my songs regularly now to the City!
88.1 FM   KNLE

Ministry in Accra, Ghana in 2018 with Pastor Oscar A. Vincent and wife Stella

January 2020 we did 30 concerts in The Philippines ! This is our band when we played at a very elaborate triple story mall ! View those concerts and my videos **on YouTube: James Willows**
1.Through Faiths Eyes
2. Runnin' on Love
3. Don't Let Go of Your Dream

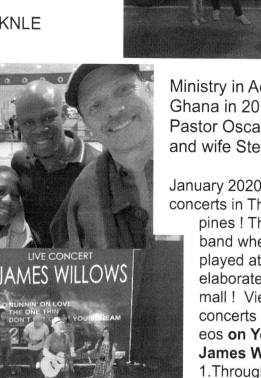

Willows HuckLand : I realize many of you got this book while visiting us at our business Willows HuckLand. I'd like to thank you for coming ! In 1993 I could not pay the bills as a full time missionary so we began the business in the gravel floored carport of my old UGLY 10 by 50 trailer.

God blessed it from the start but it was a block away from the Highway so very vulnerable. I was praying and fasting for property but was basically broke but after prayer I was mowing my lawn. I picked up a few rocks and tossed them across the street into the field. God said, "don't so that" I replied, "ya I know I shouldn't throw rocks on someone elses property." God replied, "you are going to own that property and then you will just have to pick them back up!" It seemed impossible to buy the 300 feet of Highway frontage but soon a realtors sign went up on it and I talked to the owner and made them an offer if they would finance it and I bought it for $145,000. (Lots of work to pay for it) Then in around 2010 God spoke to me, "Now is the time to build and put the design in my heart." It worked ! You can read the whole story in the book that details the formula God gave me for business success, *"Prosper In Challenging Times" Also sold on Amazon.* (Author James Willows)

By His Grace I am still in 2020 Loving Jesus

Loving my awesome wife Mary

Doing my best to love people.

The Greatest of these is LOVE

Singing at Prison 1993 with my friend Monty Christensen of PRISON IMPACT

My son graduated from Wharton yesterday May 18, 2020 ! I pray this book reaches someone before their potential is derailed like mine was ! God Bless YOU REAL GOOD !

ABE WILLOWS
LAKE TRAVIS HS
TEXAS

Made in the USA
Middletown, DE
30 May 2024